The *Complete Guide* to CHINESE HOROSCOPES

Zheng Weijian

Translated by Cao Jianxin

Better Link Press

This book is edited and designed by the Editorial Committee of *Cultural China* series.

Text: Zheng Weijian
Translation: Cao Jianxin
Designer: Wang Wei
Photos: Getty Images, Quanjing, Cultural Relics Press

Copy Editor: Susan Luu Xiang
Editor: Wu Yuezhou
Editorial Director: Zhang Yicong

Senior Consultants: Sun Yong, Wu Ying, Yang Xinci
Managing Director and Publisher: Wang Youbu

ISBN: 978-1-60220-153-8

Address any comments about *The Complete Guide to Chinese Horoscopes* to:

Better Link Press
99 Park Ave
New York, NY 10016
USA

or

Shanghai Press and Publishing Development Co., Ltd.
F 7 Donghu Road, Shanghai, China (200031)
Email: comments_betterlinkpress@hotmail.com

Printed in China by Shenzhen Donnelley Printing Co., Ltd.
5   7   9   10   8   6   4

The content in this book is provided for informational and entertainment purposes only.

Contents

Appendix

Introduction

Western astrology practices divination through the observation of the movements of planets. This has been a part of the popular culture in the west since the beginning of time; when men first glanced upwards to the evening sky at the vast constellation of stars. Likewise, the 12 symbolic animal signs (the Chinese zodiac animals) that represent the year of a person's birth are very much a part of the Chinese culture as well as in other Asian countries. Where Western astrology can predict personality traits, career paths, marriage and the attainment of wealth from planetary shifts, Eastern people can also make a wide range of accurate predictions using animal signs.

Fundamentally speaking, the animal signs of the east have a close association with Western astrology. For instance, the Rat corresponds to Aquarius. The Ox corresponds to Capricorn. The Tiger corresponds to Sagittarius. The Rabbit corresponds to Scorpio. The parameters that are used to process an individual's personal animal sign is a bit more complex than the parameters used in Western astrology, because the animal signs also take into consideration the hour, the day, the month, and the year of one's birth.

The success of each person depends on their own unique path in life and, in addition to great differences in personalities, there are a diversity of environments to consider. However, those who enjoy success seem to have similar traits that are associated with the animal signs, and also share a combination of mental acumen, initiative, respect for others, their role in society and harmonious relationship with the environment.

The twelve animals signs are inspired by eleven animals of the earth, the Rat, the Ox, the Tiger, the Rabbit, the Snake, the Horse, the Sheep, the Monkey, the Rooster, the Dog and the Pig and the Dragon, the only ancient mystical being. As extremely important elements in folk culture, these twelve animals are well known among all Chinese people. Though their exact origins cannot be confirmed, they have been passed on from generation to generation due to their popularity, convenience and amusement. They are precious heritages of practical values left by people in ancient times.

The common belief is that a person's personality and luck are more or less associated with the habits, appearance, and movements of a particular animal sign, because *sheng* (生) means "birth" and *xiao* (肖) means "similarity." *Shengxiao*, i.e. animal signs symbolize similarity between a person and a certain animal. Linking human wisdom, strength, courage, health, and charm with certain animals demonstrates a strong awareness of the influence of nature in the cycle of life that has contributed to a civilization's longevity for thousands of years.

There are various myths and legends about the origin of the twelve animal signs. The most popular legend tale is of the Yellow Emperor, who wanted twelve different kinds of animals to be on duty in Heaven at all times. He devised a competition where the Rat, the Ox, the Tiger, and the other nine animals emerged as victors. One myth attributes the origin of the twelve animal signs to a primitive society that worshipped individual animal totems belonging to specific clans. Lastly, astronomy has always been a big influence; the twenty-eight constellations in the sky corresponds to twelve periods of time. Each constellation is named after an animal. A particular commonly seen animal on duty in each period of time was then chosen to represent a certain year.

Since the time of Emperor Shun, China has been applying annals marked by a combination of the ten symbols of Heavenly Stems with the twelve symbols of Earthly Branches. The ten symbols of Heavenly Stems refer to *Jia* (甲), *Yi* (乙), *Bing* (丙), *Ding* (丁), *Wu* (戊), *Ji* (己), *Geng* (庚), *Xin* (辛), *Ren* (壬), and *Gui* (癸). The twelve symbols of Earthly Branches refer to *Zi* (子), *Chou* (丑), *Yin* (寅), *Mao* (卯), *Chen* (辰), *Si* (巳), *Wu* (午), *Wei* (未), *Shen* (申), *You* (酉), *Xu* (戌), and *Hai* (亥). There are sixty groups that are set analogically in order with a combination of the ten symbols of Heavenly Stems with the twelve symbols of Earthly Branches, such as *Jia* with *Zi* (甲子), *Yi* with *Chou* (乙 丑), and *Bing* with *Yin* (丙 寅). These sixty groups are coupled with the year and there is a repeat once every sixty years. If coupled with the month, there is a repeat once every sixty months (five years). If coupled with the day, there is a repeat once every sixty days. If coupled with the hour, there is a repeat once every sixty periods of time (i.e. a period of time stands for two hours). Such repeating goes on all the time. The year, the month, the day, and the hour are respectively marked by annals of Heavenly Stems and Earthly Branches. People in ancient times also used the twelve animals to match the twelve symbols of Earthly Branches. *Zi* stands for the Rat and *Chou* stands for the Ox, etc., with the rest of them matched analogically.

The earliest written record about the twelve animal signs can be seen in the *Book of Song (Shi Jing)*, the first poetry collection in the world. At what instance was the twelve animal signs mentioned? According to historical data, such mention took place in the Han Dynasty (206 BC–220), based on *On Balance— Materials*, a noted work by Wang Chong in the Eastern Han Dynasty (25–220). As it goes: "*Yin* stands for the Wood and the animal concerned is the Tiger. *Xu* stands for the Earth and the animal concerned is the Dog ... *Wu* stands for the Horse. *Zi* stands for the Rat. *You* stands for the Rooster. *Mao* stands for the Rabbit ... . *Hai* stands for the Pig. *Wei* stands for the Sheep. *Chou* stands for the Ox ... *Si* stands for the Snake. *Shen* stands for the Monkey."

The above-mentioned quotation only includes 11 kinds of animals, with the absence of the Dragon. However, with "The Wu Kingdom lies in *Chen* positioned at the Dragon" written in the *Spring and Autumn of Wu Yue* by Zhao Ye in the Eastern Han Dynasty, the *Chen* Dragon came into being, thus bringing about the twelve animal signs as we know it today.

The twelve animal signs were widely used in the Northern and Southern Dynasties (420–598). A letter from Yu Wenhu's mother to him that was recorded in *History of Northern Dynasty— Biography of Yu Wenhu* reads: "Two of your brothers were born at

Wuchuan Town. According to the twelve animal signs, the elder one belongs to the Rat, the younger one belongs to the Rabbit, and you belong to the Snake."

As apparent from the above, at that time, the twelve animal signs were commonly used by people to record the year of a person's birth.

However, as seen from over 1,000 bamboo slips with writing excavated from the No. 11 Qin Tomb at Shuihudi, Yunmeng in Hubei Province in 1975, *Sunrise—The Robber* clearly records the practice of divination of the robber's appearance based on the twelve animal signs. The emergence of this proves that the twelve animal signs were used even in the Spring-Autumn and Warring States periods (770–221 BC) in China. The No. 11 Qin Tomb, as investigated and proved through research, was built in the 30th year of Emperor Qin's reign in 217 BC. With some slight differences, the arrangement of the animal names, Heavenly Stems, and Earthly Branches are generally similar to that of the twelve animal signs that became popular later. The divination process and the logical application are also similar to those of the twelve animals signs. Therefore, it can be deduced that the twelve animal signs matching Heavenly Stems and Earthly Branches appearing on the bamboo slips excavated at Shuihudi were the initial patterns of the twelve animal signs later.

The popularity of the twelve animal signs, which reveals the wisdom of people in ancient China, derives a lot from traditional Chinese culture with a significant impact on its cultural foundation. This is not only a vivid way of recording, but also an appealing aspect of folk culture that has been handed down through a period of over 2,000 years, forming the basic characteristics of each animal. For instance, a person born in a Rat year is bright and wealthy, a person born in an Ox year is diligent and down-to-earth, a person born in a Tiger year is robust and fierce, a person born in a Rabbit year is quiet and agile, a person born in a Dragon year is extraordinary and attractive, a person born in a Snake year is romantic and mysterious, a person born in a Horse year is uninhibited, a person born in a Sheep year is mild and elegant, a person born in a Monkey year is smart and lively, a person born in a Rooster year is spirited and lucky, a person born in a Dog year is faithful and fierce, and finally, a person born in a Pig year is honest, lazy, and happy. They influence and enrich the daily life of people.

The twelve animal signs representing the year of a person's birth figures significantly in *The Book of Changes* (*Yi Jing*), Five Elements, yin and yang, Eight Diagrams, Heavenly Stems, and Earthly Branches. This book provides an insight into the common trends in one's life, personality, profession, love and marriage, and luck of wealth.

What Is My Animal Sign?

The twelve animal signs are different from the signs of Western astrology. The signs of the Western astrology is defined by the month, while the twelve animal signs are determined by the year. However, the year is marked by two kinds of calendars in China, i.e. the solar calendar that is used universally in the world, such as 2015, and the lunar calendar, which is a form of recording unique to China. The lunar calendar is represented by twelve animal signs, such as 2015 as the year of the Sheep. Those born in this year belong to the Sheep.

Particular attention should be paid that a day before and after February 4 (solar calendar) is the starting day of the animal sign, because the day before and after February 4 is the "Beginning of Spring" in the 24 seasonal periods of the Chinese lunar calendar. The beginning of the animal sign is decided by the "Beginning of Spring" according to the Chinese lunar calendar. For instance, the starting time for a baby born in 2015 as a Sheep is neither the zero hour of January 1, 2015 (solar calendar), nor the zero hour of the first day of the first lunar month of 2015 (i.e. February 19, 2015 according to the solar calendar), but 11:58 AM of February 4, 2015 according to the solar calendar (i.e. the 16th day of the 12th lunar month of 2014 according to lunar calendar), because this is the time for the "Beginning of Spring" of 2015.

The overall fortunes for each animal sign are decided by the day of birth and related month according to the lunar calendar. For reference, please convert the day of birth of solar calendar into the day of birth of lunar calendar. The lunar calendar is usually about one month later than the time of the solar calendar. For an accurate date, two methods can be used for conversion; one is to consult the permanent calendar, and the other is to calculate based on the following formula. Such calculation may occasionally have a slight difference, but will not influence results in most cases.

Assume: The year of the solar calendar − 1977 (or 1901) = 4Q + R

The result: The date of the lunar calendar = 14Q + 10.6 (R + 1) + the serial number of the date within the year − 29.5n (Note: Q, R and n are all natural numbers, R < 4)

For instance: What is the date of the lunar calendar in comparison with May 7, 1994 of the solar calendar?

1994 − 1977 = 17 = 4 × 4 + 1

Therefore: Q = 4, R = 1

The date of the lunar calendar in comparison with May 7, 1994 of the solar calendar should be as follows:

14 × 4 + 10.6 (1 + 1) + (31 + 28 + 31 + 30 + 7) − 29.5n = 204.2 − 29.5n

Then 204.2 divided by 29.5 equals 6 as the quotient. 6 is the value of n and the remainder is 27.2. 27 is the 27th day of the lunar calendar. Taking into account that the lunar calendar is about one month later than the solar calendar, it should be the 27th day of the third lunar month.

In the process of calculating the serial number of the date of birth (solar calendar) in a year, there are 31 days in January, March, May, July, August, October, and December, and 30 days in April, June, September, and November, and 28 days in February (29 days in the leap year). Then how do you determine the number of days in February? Is it 28 days or 29 days? If the number of the year can be divided by 4, then there will be 29 days in February in this year. If it cannot be divided by 4, then there will be 28 days in this year. For instance, in February 2000, $2000 \div 4 = 500$. Therefore, there were 29 days in February 2000; in February 2001, $2001 \div 4 = 500 + 1$. Therefore, there were 28 days in February 2001.

A day was divided into twelve periods of time in ancient China and each period of time amounted to two hours. For convenience, hours will be directly used as indication in the following part.

The Compatibility

The supportive and destructive relationship among the twelve animal signs is shown by the relationship between the superior and the subordinate, the cooperative relationship in business and work as well as in marriage. For instance, if a Rat person wants to seek more business or a better job, which animal sign is supposed to be suitable to help him? According to the Chinese twelve animal signs, he should align with the Dragon, the Monkey, or the Ox, thus enjoying career growth.

Compared with the Western astrological signs, compatibility based on the twelve animal signs is more beneficial in marriage. For instance, if a man's animal sign is the Rat, then a woman of the Dragon, or the Monkey, or the Ox is more suitable as his spouse, because the matching of these symbols can bring heart-to-heart harmony, wealth, easy access to success, and happiness all their life.

For thousands of years, there has been the determination of marriage based on the related animal signs among the common folks in China. In the past, both sides must provide the fortune-teller with their dates of birth including the hour, the day, the month, and the year (commonly called Eight Characters), to figure out if their animal signs were suitable for marriage. This was important. It would be suitable if they were in a mutually supportive relationship.

The compatibility of the twelve animal signs chiefly references the concepts of Three Harmony and Six Harmony. Three Harmony and Six Harmony are marked by combination of the power of the several kinds of elements in the Five Elements (i.e. Metal, Wood, Water, Fire, and Earth). Six Harmony is like the relationship between the husband and wife, while Three Harmony is like the affection between the mother and child.

Three Harmony represents perfect compatibility, i.e. three kinds of animal signs make an auspicious match. There are four groups of auspicious matches; those of the Monkey, the Rat, and

Three-Harmony Group of
Monkey, Rat and Dragon

Three-Harmony Group of Snake,
Rooster and Ox

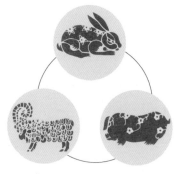

Three-Harmony Group of
Rabbit, Sheep and Pig

Three-Harmony Group of
Tiger, Horse and Dog

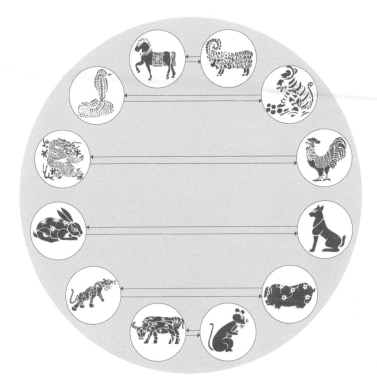

Six Harmony

the Dragon in one group; the Snake, the Rooster, and the Ox in another; the Rabbit, the Sheep and the Pig, in one group; the Tiger, the Horse, and the Dog the last group. The Three Harmony concept is the result of many years of research. Their ability to get along with each other, their ideas, values, habits, and mannerisms are all very well matched.

Six Harmony refers to hidden charity, implying a benefactor who helps you without your knowledge. It is not the combination of six animal signs, but the integration of two animal signs as a group. Therefore, there are six groups of benefactors; the Rat and the Ox; the Tiger and the Pig; the Rabbit and the Dog; the Dragon and the Rooster; the Snake and the Monkey; the Horse and the Sheep.

The Rat
- With the Dragon: The Dragon, full of vigor, brings a lot of joy to the Rat and the Rat's praises strokes the Dragon's ego.
- With the Monkey: The Rat enjoys the Monkey's cleverness. If the Monkey is sincere towards the Rat, they will get along with each other well.
- With the Ox: The mild Ox can bring out the best in the Rat, giving the latter a sense of comfort.

The Ox
- With the Rat: The enthusiastic Rat can bring joy to the silent Ox and be faithful to the Ox, hence the two get along well with each other.
- With the Snake: If the Snake is faithful to the Ox, it can develop the career with its talent.
- With the Rooster: The Ox, with the desire to lead, can bring the conservative Rooster under its control, getting from each other what they need.

The Tiger
- With the Pig: They are attracted to each other and will please each other while enjoying a happy life.
- With the Horse: It is easy for the Horse to attract the attention of the Tiger. They will be very happy, having mutual respect and support each other.
- With the Dog: The conceited Tiger displays its mildness only in the presence of the faithful Dog. The Tiger can also encourage the Dog to pursue his goals. They take care of each other and share the good and the bad.

The Rabbit
- With the Sheep: The Sheep is not so independent. The Rabbit enjoys taking care of its lovers and they get along well with each other.
- With the Dog: They both wish to live in peace and work hard together for the future.

- With the Pig: They have similar characters and enjoy tranquility. They are attracted to each other and are affectionate.

The Dragon
- With the Rat: Unrestrained Dragon would be moved by the praises of the Rat and it also enjoys the down-to-earth manner and humor of the Rat.
- With the Monkey: Both of them are creative, however, the Monkey has to be careful not to play tricks on the Dragon.
- With the Rooster: The Rooster worships the Dragon. When the Dragon comes across set-backs, the Rooster would faithfully encourage the Dragon.

The Snake
- With the Ox: The Snake would be attracted by the determination in the Ox's eyes, but they will have quarrels every once in a while.
- With the Monkey: They are very well matched. Therefore, it is the best for a Snake person to marry a Monkey person.
- With the Rooster: Despite arguments, the more they argue, the more they get along and become attached. For them, arguing is a way of communication.

The Horse
- With the Tiger: The noble and generous Tiger enables the Horse to serve and the Horse can also get sincere affection from the Tiger.
- With the Sheep: The Horse can be easily attracted by the tenderness of the Sheep. The Horse feels happy with the sentimental attachment of the Sheep.
- With the Dog: The smart Dog helps the Horse to develop its career. The Horse would appreciate and thrive with such a supportive partner.

The Sheep
- With the Rabbit: The Sheep, lacking independence, can rely on

the Rabbit, who has the ability to make money. This match can work out very well.

- With the Horse: The Horse is very willing to help the Sheep. The artistic ambitions of the Sheep can satisfy the noble temperament of the Horse.
- With the Pig: Both of them are mild and they are attracted to each other. The Pig would fight for the Sheep when the latter experience a set-back.

The Monkey
- With the Rat: The Rat knows how to please the Monkey. Their life is full of joy when they live together.
- With the Dragon: The energetic Dragon brings joy to the Monkey, captivating the Monkey all the time. The Dragon is always a winner in love affairs. It is only the Monkey that knows how to defeat the Dragon.

The Rooster
- With the Ox: The faithful Ox gets along well with the conservative rooster. They will have a steady relationship with a lot of affection.
- With the Dragon: The enthusiastic Rooster never minds standing behind the Dragon. The Rooster is proud of the achievements of the Dragon.
- With the Snake: They discuss life together to seek inspiration and motivation. They are perfectly matched.

The Dog
- With the Tiger: The Dog, with unnecessary worries, gets strong support from the Tiger. The Tiger also needs the faithfulness of the Dog.
- With the Rabbit: The careful Rabbit would support the Dog while the Dog also likes the kind Rabbit.
- With the Horse: They understand the needs of each other and respect each other.

The Pig

- With the Tiger: They are attracted to each other and know how to please each other. They make the best match.
- With the Rabbit: The Rabbit is attracted by the wisdom of the Pig. The enthusiasm of the Pig can also excite the careful Rabbit.
- With the Sheep: This is the best marriage. The Sheep makes the Pig feel safe.

The Five Elements

According to traditional Chinese culture, the world is composed of Five Elements, i.e. Metal, Wood, Water, Fire, and Earth. There are supportive and destructive relationships among them, i.e. Wood generates Fire, Fire generates Earth, Earth generates Metal, Metal generates Water, Water generates Wood. This supportive cycle is mutually beneficial. At the same time, there are destructive relationships among them, i.e. Wood subdues Earth, Earth subdues Water, Water subdues Fire, Fire subdues Metal, Metal subdues Wood. The destructive cycle brings about mutual harm and disadvantages.

The supportive relationship of the Five Elements is like the mother giving birth to the son, showing support, and representing balance and good luck. The destructive relationship of the Five Elements is like a war, symbolizing mutual hostility.

The supportive relationship of the Five Elements is expressed by following; Wood generates Fire: Since Wood is used as fuel, when Wood is burnt out, Fire would die automatically. Fire generates Earth: Objects burnt out by Fire would turn into ash which is the Earth. Earth generates Metal: Metal is within the Earth and stones and cannot be extracted unless it is smelted. Metal generates Water: Metal, after having been burnt, would turn into liquid which is Water. Water needs to be guided by the metal-ware. Water generates Wood: Water can irrigate trees, making them lush.

The destructive relationship of the Five Elements is expressed by following; Wood subdues the Earth: Without plants, there will be water loss and soil erosion. Fire subdues Metal: Fierce Fire can melt Metal. Earth subdues Water: Earth can cover Water. Metal subdues Wood: Metal cutters can saw trees. Water subdues Fire: Water can put out Fire.

Among the twelve animal signs, Wood corresponds to the Tiger and the Rabbit; Fire corresponds to the Horse and the Snake; Water corresponds to the Rat and the Pig; Metal corresponds to the Monkey and the Rooster; Earth corresponds to the Ox, the Dragon, the Sheep and the Dog.

Observing and getting to know the twelve animal signs serve to recognize the original idea of ancient people in establishing them. Later, common folks in China divided these animal signs into yin and yang so as to correspond to the Five Elements. There are also supportive and destructive relationships within yin, yang and the Five Elements of the twelve animal signs. It is shown as follows:

Twelve Animal Signs	Years of Twelve Animal Signs	Twelve Symbols of Earthly Branches	Yin & Yang and Five Elements
Rat	The year of the Rat	The year of *Zi*	Yang Water
Ox	The year of the Ox	The year of *Chou*	Yin Earth
Tiger	The year of the Tiger	The year of *Yin*	Yang Wood
Rabbit	The year of the Rabbit	The year of *Mao*	Yin Wood
Dragon	The year of the Dragon	The year of *Chen*	Yang Earth
Snake	The year of the Snake	The year of *Si*	Yin Fire
Horse	The year of the Horse	The year of *Wu*	Yang Fire
Sheep	The year of the Sheep	The year of *Wei*	Yin Earth
Monkey	The year of the Monkey	The year of *Shen*	Yang Metal
Rooster	The year of the Rooster	The year of *You*	Yin Metal
Dog	The year of the Dog	The year of *Xu*	Yang Earth
Pig	The year of the Pig	The year of *Hai*	Yin Water

The Colors

The twelve animal signs have their lucky and unlucky colors. We can seek benefits and avoid harm if we are able to make use of these colors in our daily life and work. For instance, Rat people are associated with Water according to the Five Elements. Their own colors are black and blue while white, apricot, red, and purple are colors also suitable for them. Yellow, orange, light green, and green are not lucky colors for them.

Zi (Rat)—Water
Water = Water: black and blue (Water √).
Metal generates Water: white and apricot (Metal √).
Water subdues Fire: red and purple (Fire ×).
Earth subdues Water: yellow and orange (Earth ×).
Water generates Wood: cyan and green (Wood ×).

Chou (Ox)—Earth
Earth = Earth: yellow and orange (Earth √).
Fire generates Earth: red and purple (Fire √).
Earth subdues Water: black and blue (Water ×).
Wood subdues Earth: cyan and green (Wood ×).
Earth generates Metal: white and apricot (Metal ×).

Yin (Tiger)—Wood
Wood = Wood: cyan and green (Wood √).
Water generates Wood: black and blue (Water √).
Wood subdues Earth: yellow and orange (Earth ×).
Metal subdues Wood: white and apricot (Metal ×).
Wood generates Fire: red and purple (Fire ×).

Mao (Rabbit)—Wood
Wood = Wood: cyan and green (Wood √).
Water generates Wood: black and blue (Water √).
Wood subdues Earth: yellow and orange (Earth ×).
Metal subdues Wood: white and apricot (Metal ×).

Wood generates Fire: red and purple (Fire ×).

Chen (Dragon)—Earth

Earth = Earth: yellow and orange (Earth √).
Fire generates Earth: red and purple (Fire √).
Earth subdues Water: black and blue (Water ×).
Wood subdues Earth: cyan and green (Wood ×).
Earth generates Metal: white and apricot (Metal ×).

Si (Snake)—Fire

Fire = Fire: red and purple (Fire √).
Wood generates Fire: cyan and green (Wood √).
Fire subdues Metal: white and apricot (Metal ×).
Water subdues Fire: black and blue (Water ×).
Fire generates Earth: yellow and orange (Earth ×).

Wu (Horse)—Fire

Fire = Fire: red and purple (Fire √).
Wood generates Fire: cyan and green (Wood √).
Fire subdues Metal: white and apricot (Metal ×).
Water subdues Fire: black and blue (Water ×).
Fire generates Earth: yellow and orange (Earth ×).

Wei (Sheep)—Earth

Earth = Earth: yellow and orange (Earth √).
Fire generates Earth: red and purple (Fire √).
Earth subdues Water: black and blue (Water ×).
Wood subdues Earth: cyan and green (Wood ×).
Earth generates Metal: white and apricot (Metal ×).

Shen (Monkey)—Metal

Metal = Metal: white and apricot (Metal √).
Earth generates Metal: yellow and orange (Earth √).
Metal subdues Wood: cyan and green (Wood ×).
Fire subdues Metal: red and purple (Fire ×).
Metal generates Water: black and blue (Water ×).

You (Rooster)—Metal
> Metal = Metal: white and apricot (Metal √).
> Earth generates Metal: yellow and orange (Earth √).
> Metal subdues Wood: cyan and green (Wood ×).
> Fire subdues Metal: red and purple (Fire ×).
> Metal generates Water: black and blue (Water ×).

Xu (Dog)—Earth
> Earth = Earth: yellow and orange (Earth √).
> Fire generates Earth: red and purple (Fire √).
> Earth subdues Water: black and blue (Water ×).
> Wood subdues Earth: cyan and green (Wood ×).
> Earth generates Metal: white and apricot (Metal ×).

Hai (Pig)—Water
> Water = Water: black and blue (Water √).
> Metal generates Water: white and apricot (Metal √).
> Water subdues Fire: red and purple (Fire ×).
> Earth subdues Water: yellow and orange (Earth ×).
> Water generates Wood: cyan and green (Wood ×).

The Numbers

The twelve animal signs not only have their colors and directions, but also their corresponding numbers and numbers that are lucky and unlucky. For instance, the numbers of Rat people are 1 and 6. Numbers 4, 9, 1, and 6 are suitable for them, whereas 5, 0, 3, and 8 are unlucky.

Zi (Rat)—1 and 6
> Water = Water: 1 and 6 (√).
> Metal generates Water: 4 and 9 (√).
> Water subdues Fire: 2 and 7 (×).
> Earth subdues Water: 5 and 0 (×).
> Water generates Wood: 3 and 8 (×).

Chou (Ox)—5 and 0
    Earth = Earth: 5 and 0 (√).
    Fire generates Earth: 2 and 7 (√).
    Earth subdues Water: 1 and 6 (×).
    Wood subdues Earth: 3 and 8 (×).
    Earth generates Metal: 4 and 9 (×).

Yin (Tiger)—3 and 8
    Wood = Wood: 3 and 8 (√).
    Water generates Wood: 1 and 6 (√).
    Wood subdues Earth: 5 and 0 (×).
    Metal subdues Wood: 4 and 9 (×).
    Wood generates Fire: 2 and 7 (×).

Mao (Rabbit)—3 and 8
    Wood = Wood: 3 and 8 (√).
    Water generates Wood: 1 and 6 (√).
    Wood subdues Earth: 5 and 0 (×).
    Metal subdues Wood: 4 and 9 (×).
    Wood generates Fire: 2 and 7 (×).

Chen (Dragon)—5 and 0
    Earth = Earth: 5 and 0 (√).
    Fire generates Earth: 2 and 7 (√).
    Earth subdues Water: 1 and 6 (×).
    Wood subdues Earth: 3 and 8 (×).
    Earth generates Metal: 4 and 9 (×).

Si (Snake)—2 and 7
    Fire = Fire: 2 and 7 (√).
    Wood generates Fire: 3 and 8 (√).
    Fire subdues Metal: 4 and 9 (×).
    Water subdues Fire: 1 and 6 (×).
    Fire generates Earth: 5 and 0 (×).

Wu (Horse)—2 and 7
  Fire = Fire: 2 and 7 (√).
  Wood generates Fire: 3 and 8 (√).
  Fire subdues Metal: 4 and 9 (×).
  Water subdues Fire: 1 and 6 (×).
  Fire generates Earth: 5 and 0 (×).

Wei (Sheep)—5 and 0
  Fire = Fire: 5 and 0 (√)
  Fire generates Earth: 2 and 7 (√).
  Earth subdues Water: 1 and 6 (×).
  Wood subdues Earth: 3 and 8 (×).
  Earth generates Metal: 4 and 9 (×).

Shen (Monkey)—4 and 9
  Metal = Metal: 4 and 9 (√).
  Earth generates Metal: 5 and 0 (√).
  Metal subdues Mood: 3 and 8 (×).
  Fire subdues Metal: 2 and 7 (×).
  Metal generates Water: 1 and 6 (×).

You (Rooster)—4 and 9
  Metal = Metal: 4 and 9 (√).
  Earth generates Metal: 5 and 0 (√).
  Metal subdues Wood: 3 and 8 (×).
  Fire subdues Metal: 2 and 7 (×).
  Metal generates Water: 1 and 6 (×).

Xu (Dog)—5 and 0
  Earth = Earth: 5 and 0 (√).
  Fire generates Earth: 2 and 7 (√).
  Earth subdues Water: 1 and 6 (×).
  Wood subdues Earth: 3 and 8 (×).
  Earth generates Metal: 4 and 9 (×).

Hai (Pig)—1 and 6

    Water = Water: 1 and 6 ($\checkmark$).

    Metal generates Water: 4 and 9 ($\checkmark$).

    Water subdues Fire: 2 and 7 (×).

    Earth subdues Water: 5 and 0 (×).

    Water generates Wood: 3 and 8 (×).

The Directions

The twelve animal signs not only have their colors, but also their corresponding directions.

Twelve Animal Signs	Corresponding Direction	Suitable Directions
Rat	The north	The north and the west
Ox	The north-east	The north-east and the south
Tiger	The east	The north and the east
Rabbit	The east	The north and the east
Dragon	The south-east	The south and the south-east
Snake	The south-east	The south and the east
Horse	The south	The south and the east
Sheep	The south-west	The south and the south-west
Monkey	The south-west	The south-west and the west
Rooster	The west	The west and the north-west
Dog	The north-west	The north-west and the south
Pig	The north-west	The north and the west

Chapter One
The Rat

The first among all the twelve animal signs, the Rat represents wisdom. It possesses a special kind of intelligence, a combination of street smarts and intuition that the other animals don't have. For instance, the mouse in the *Tom and Jerry* cartoons always outwits the cat and escapes from him. The Rat has a strong ability to quickly adapt to adverse conditions and overcome the ups and downs of life.

Lunar Years of the Rat in the Solar Calendar

5 February 1912 to 3 February 1913

5 February 1924 to 3 February 1925

5 February 1936 to 3 February 1937

5 February 1948 to 3 February 1949

5 February 1960 to 3 February 1961

5 February 1972 to 3 February 1973

4 February 1984 to 3 February 1985

4 February 1996 to 3 February 1997

4 February 2008 to 2 February 2009

4 February 2020 to 2 February 2021

4 February 2032 to 2 February 2033

4 February 2044 to 2 February 2045

Life Path

People who are born in the year of the Rat can adapt to any environment. They are popular in their social circles because they are not particular or pessimistic. Because of their easy-going nature, others are generally glad to help the Rat out. Sharp-eyed, they know a good opportunity when they see one and do not hesitate to grab on to it and turn it into a success. They are absolutely sure about what they want and are willing to overcome any challenge to get it. As natural-born optimists, they enjoy more happiness in life. They need to continue to maintain the effort to get along with others. In doing so, they will be able to successfully coast through life.

Personality

Rats are clever, smart, quick-minded, funny, observant, and easy to get along with. They are hard-working, diligent, enterprising, and firm, with a tenacity for survival and a very flexible adaptability. Tiny as they are, they are indomitable and work quietly. They never give up for the sake of their career, family, and objectives. People born in the year of the Rat are kind, open-minded, joyful, and sociable. They value their relationship with family and friends, holding a deep sentimental attachment to them. They prefer gatherings and parties, not only as a participant but also as the organizer. On many occasions, they can liven the atmosphere and make others laugh with their great sense of humor. However, they need to overcome their stubbornness and maintain their poise at the sight of profit.

Profession

Thanks to their intuition and sharp observational skills, the Rat is suited to engaged in work that involves meticulous craftsmanship or a high level of caution. At the same time, they are active and independent. Therefore, work that doesn't require much supervision is ideal for them. However, it is not wise for them to get involved in politics-related work.

Love and Marriage

Most people born in the year of the Rat put great value in love. They are very kind and forgiving toward those they hold dear. When arguing with their lovers, they are the first to give in. Therefore, when they interact with the opposite sex, it is very easy for them to be favored. Their principle about love is: "The giver is happier than the receiver." As a result, they are not as frustrated when a relationship doesn't work out. It is ideal for them to pair with the Dragon, the Monkey, and the Ox, which will lead to true rapport, wealth, and happiness. They are likely to have conflicts with the Horse, the Sheep, the Rabbit, and the Rooster. However, if they can gradually adapt to one another, they will enjoy bliss and happiness in their old age.

Marriage Compatibility with Women Born in Other Animal Years

The Rat Man with the Rat Woman: They will share a very tender kind of love.

The Rat Man with the Ox Woman: This will be a perfect match. As long as the Ox is faithful, she can always rely on the Rat to be thoughtful and affectionate.

The Rat Man with the Tiger Woman: If the Tiger can maintain realistic expectations, then their marriage will be an easy one.

The Rat Man with the Rabbit Woman: They will have complete opposite views of love and romance. The Rat may not necessarily tolerate it when the Rabbit, whether intentional or not, goes against his will.

The Rat Man with the Dragon Woman: This will be an ideal match. The Rat knows his spouse very well and will respect what

The Rat Marrying off Its Daughter to the Cat

The Jade Emperor dispatched the Cat to notify the Ox and the Tiger to be ranked in Heaven. Having overheard it from the Cat, the Rat arrived first. The muddle-headed Jade Emperor endowed the Rat as the leader of twelve animal signs, whereas the Cat was squeezed out from its place as one of the twelve animals of the Chinese zodiac, hence resulting in deep hatred between them. Intending to reconcile with the Cat, the Rat pleaded the weasel to serve as a matchmaker to marry its most beautiful daughter to the Cat. The Cat agreed satisfactorily. Therefore, the Rat chose an auspicious day, stole a tiger-head shoe to be a sedan chair which carried its daughter to the Cat's den. Consequently, the Rat's daughter was eaten by the Cat.

she thinks, hence satisfying the ego of the Dragon.

The Rat Man with the Snake Woman: The tenderness and thoughtfulness of the Rat will make life very pleasant for the Snake.

The Rat Man with the Horse Woman: Both of them are quite impulsive, so they will not likely tolerate each other well.

The Rat Man with the Sheep Woman: The Sheep is fond of the Rat's wealth and will try to control the life of the Rat.

The Rat Man with the Monkey Woman: This will be a fairly happy match. The Monkey may deceive the Rat, causing misunderstanding and hurt as result. But after a short period of time, the Rat will forgive the Monkey.

The Rat Man with the Rooster Woman: This will be a fairly happy match. The practical Rooster will be able to keep the Rat from indulging in excessive extravagance.

The Rat Man with the Dog Woman: The Dog will be happy that the Rat likes to go out frequently, which satisfies the social nature of the Dog.

The Rat Man with the Pig Woman: This will be a happy pairing. The Pig enjoys fairly good luck when it comes to wealth and doesn't mind sharing it with the Rat.

Marriage Compatibility with Men Born in Other Animal Years

The Rat Woman with the Rat Man: This match will provide mutual admiration for both.

The Rat Woman with the Ox Man: This will be a peaceful and happy match.

The Rat Woman with the Tiger Man: As long as the Rat can tolerate the sometimes risky behavior of the Tiger, there will be no aggravation in their love.

The Rat Woman with the Rabbit Man: The overly social nature of the Rabbit will likely cause him to overlook his wife.

The Rat Woman with the Dragon Man: This will be a very happy match. The Rat will not mind sacrificing her own interests in order to help the Dragon further his career.

The Rat Woman with the Snake Man: The Rat in love is

often overwhelmed by affection, readily believing the Snake. Of course, the Snake also lacks rational consideration.

The Rat Woman with the Horse Man: This will not be a happy match, because they are constantly at odds with each other.

The Rat Woman with the Sheep Man: This will not be an ideal marriage.

The Rat Woman with the Monkey Man: This will be a perfect match. They will share a sweet love and happy marriage.

The Rat Woman with the Rooster Man: Their life together will not be a happy one. They will quarrel all day long with no peace in the family at any time.

The Rat Woman with the Dog Man: This will be an ideal match. The Dog is very tender towards the Rat.

The Rat Woman with the Pig Man: This will be a happy marriage. However, the Rat should not to be too uninhibited, because this will put off the pig.

The Luck of Wealth

People born in the Rat year are fond of saving and collecting. They're motivated by the fear of not having enough to eat or not having a roof over their heads. Because of this, they will accumulate a handsome amount of savings in middle age. Their thrifty and conservative nature means that they prefer to put their money in the bank for a moderate, yet stable return so they're sure to lead a comfortable and happy life.

Overall Fortunes of the Rat in Different Animal Years

The Year of the Rat: This will be a busy year that might involve a significant vertical career move. Bid the end of the year a quiet farewell by avoiding travel.

The Year of the Ox: This will be a calm and smooth year with neither any loss or gain. Instead, family and friends will be the ones to gain a lot.

The Year of the Tiger: This is the year to see career growth on many levels that might involve moving to another city or region. If so, this can mean more hard work that will be followed by award and recognition. Bigger gains will follow if caution is taken to pursue them.

The Year of the Rabbit: There will be both good luck and bad luck. Troubles can lead to disasters. Therefore, one should do more kind things to generate good karma.

The Year of the Dragon: This is the year of smooth sailing when it comes to the pursuit of wealth, career and study. However, one should be mindful of people with ulterior motives and be very careful when making friends, so as to prevent jealousy and envy.

The Year of the Snake: This is not an ideal year, but there is an auspicious star shining over as it happens. Less contact with places known for gain and fame can turn bad luck into good luck, reduce the possibility of disasters, and keep one's health up.

The Year of the Horse: Both the male and female Rat should be careful and fly under the radar this year. They should develop careers or pursue fame and recognition in order to come up against the adversity.

The Year of the Sheep: All career goals can be realized this year as long as one works for them. There will some obstacles but not any serious set-backs. Be careful not to get into any heated arguments or debates. If you're in the right, be lenient towards the other party.

The Year of the Monkey: Be cautious when making friends. At the end of the year, one should work harder for success.

The Year of the Rooster: Everything has promise and potential this year. Therefore, one should advance steadily to prevent from being carried away by success.

The Year of the Dog: There is significant increase in recognition this year, though it will come without wealth (i.e., a promotion without the raise to go with it). Do not travel to dangerous places. At the end of the year, there will be good luck which should not be taken for granted.

The Year of the Pig: Thanks to an auspicious star, there will be more gains than losses, more luck than misfortunes. Take care to be mindful of one's health.

Overall Fortunes of the Rat Born in Different Months by the Lunar Calendar

The 1st Lunar Month: They lead a comfortable life without hard work thanks to past and present efforts of family and spouse.

The 2nd Lunar Month: There will be twists and turns. Even if they are kind, attractive, and talented, their conservative nature prevents them from accomplishing much.

The 3rd Lunar Month: Their kindness will be tested and they will experience a lot anguish. They could go through a period of slight depression.

The 4th Lunar Month: Don't expect any help or support from family. They could be the subject of discrimination. However, depending on the hour of their birth, things will look up.

The 5th Lunar Month: They will work hard and enjoy help from others. Their career will proceed smoothly despite hardship. In middle age, they will be respected owing to the wealth they will gain from all their hard work.

The 6th Lunar Month: There will be a lack of help and support from family members. Despite support from others, their persistent health concerns will make it difficult to achieve their goals. Fortunately, because of their resolute nature, they can rise above adversity and manage to have an outstanding life.

The 7th Lunar Month: They are lucky persons who will benefit from a strong, stable family life and will always have help from others in the career. Because of this, it is easy for them to be open-minded and get along happily with everyone.

The 8th Lunar Month: With a strong family foundation, enormous help from parents, and assistance from many benefactors, they will enjoy career growth throughout life. They are smart and intelligent and enjoy a lot of admiration from people.

The 9th Lunar Month: Narrow-minded and rather timid, they are marked by the mentality of being at the mercy of fate. Despite being unsociable, they enjoy an extremely good relationship with their spouse and children. They have happy and peaceful life.

The 10th Lunar Month: They will not have much support and help from family members. However, they are very ambitious and knowledgeable. Though they will be free of any serious misfortune, they will encounter many twists and turns throughout their life.

The 11th Lunar Month: They will not have much support and help from family members. The first part of their life will be a hard one. However, they will enjoy happiness in their later years as a result of the help they will receive from others during mid-life. They are free from serious misfortunes. In mid-life, they will experience rapid development in career.

The 12th Lunar Month: With lots of heritages from ancestors, profound sentiments among brothers and sisters, deep love with the spouse and help from benefactors, one feels safe and leisurely, being able to make success quickly. Simple and honest, one is enthusiastic about helping the poor, hence being very popular among people.

Overall Fortunes of the Rat Born on Different Days by the Lunar Calendar

The 1st Day: The early years of their life will be unremarkable, but they will have help from others in mid-life that will elevate the standing.

The 2nd Day: They are kind and mild and enjoy good health. They will work hard in early years with no help from brothers. However, they will experience a change of luck in mid-life followed by prosperity in old age. Male Rats born on this day tend to be smart while female Rats are attractive.

The 3rd Day: They will have desirable spouses and their life together will be a happy one. Unfortunately, such a marriage may not last long. They will enjoy good luck in middle age.

The 4th Day: Their will enjoy a steady flow of good fortune. They are smart and eager to learn. The woman can have a nice husband while the man can have a nice wife. Their life will develop at a stable pace, experience wealth in mid-life, and enjoy old age in peace.

The 5th Day: They are smart, know the ways of the world, and take good care of their family. However, there will be a lack of help and support from family members. They will have to work hard in their early years, but they will enjoy prosperity in mid-life and stability in old age.

The 6th Day: Though they are eager to learn they will not accomplish much in the early years. They won't enjoy success until after forty years old.

The 7th Day: They have a complex personality and an unpredictable temperament. They can rely on brothers or male family members, but will have to act low-key and pursue the goals quietly to ensure success. The female Rat is luckier than the male Rate born on this day. She enjoys longevity.

The 8th Day: They are smart and will enjoy peace and happiness throughout life. However, they will have a contentious relationship with parents. Therefore, they should seek to achieve success away from home. Their success depends on their meeting the right people who can help them. Their mid-life and old age will be a content one even though it will be without outstanding wealth.

The 9th Day: Their early years will be unremarkable, but they will be quite comfortable in old age, enjoying both fame and fortune. They are kind-hearted and generous.

The 10th Day: They will find themselves in an undesirable situation in the early years. Male Rat will be emotionally attached to the wife and the son. What's more, they even heavily attached to other women and wine. They will have to work hard at a young age to create good opportunities in mid-life and enjoy happiness in old age.

The 11th Day: Their mid-life will be marked with hard work. Despite having good lucky and fortune, they will lack the ability to make good decisions. But their old age will be a happy one.

The 12th Day: With a mild, yet diligent character, they are able to bear hardship. They will not have good luck in the early years, but a change of luck will occur in mid-life and they will be happy in old age. They will enjoy both fame and fortune with a prosperous family.

The 13th Day: There will be good fortune with a lot of happiness and wealth, as well as the prospect of success.

The 14th Day: Both men and women have stable and serene characters. For male Rats, wealth and career development will come from the help of wife. For pretty female Rats, their change of luck will happen in mid-life.

The 15th Day: If fate is favorable on the hour of birth, they will enjoy profit and wealth throughout life.

The 16th Day: They are smart and fond of delving into art. Without support from family, they will work hard at young age and become proficient in art in mid-life.

The 17th Day: They are fairly intelligent, but persistent. There are no family members to rely on when they are young, resulting in self-reliance to start the career. For male Rats, after thirty-five years old, they will have good luck, find a nice wife and enjoy successful career development.

The 18th Day: Despite lots of intelligence and cleverness, they are stubborn, with no leniency towards others, hence easily stepping on people's toes. Because of contentious relationship with parents, they will have to stand on their own feet to start career.

The 19th Day: Blessed with both fame and fortune, they will enjoy a solid reputation in society. Their early years will be unremarkable, but wealth will come in old age.

The 20th Day: It is better for male Rat to leave home to seek wealth. They will not have family members and friends to rely on, but good luck will come in old age. The female Rat, who is fond of talk and laughter, will enjoy good relationships with others.

They will help husband and be very capable of taking care of the family. They live a happy life.

The 21st Day: Male Rat will have a nice wife who will be able to help to navigate the problems of daily life. In mid-life, their career will be smooth with the help of others. For the female Rat, her hard work will certainly pay off.

The 22nd Day: They are smart and true to their word. Despite hardship in early years, they will see prosperity with success in fame and fortune after thirty years old. There will be enormous happiness and wealth in old age.

The 23rd Day: They have many ways to go about doing things, changing mind frequently. There will be no development before mid-life, but happiness and wealth will come after that period and in old age. The female Rat will be luckier and will be blessed with many children.

The 24th Day: Smart, deft with hands and devoted to tasks, they will become successful persons to be respected. They will make lots of money if working away from home. The female Rat is not as lucky as male Rat and will have to work harder, but she will enjoy happiness in mid-life and old age.

The 25th Day: Simple and honest, they are fond of minding others' business and doing good deeds. The male Rat will find a nice wife to assist him throughout the life. The female Rat are diligent and will develop her career in mid-life and old age, having a prosperous family along the way.

The 26th Day: Benevolent and carefree, they will enjoy sweetness after tasting bitterness. There will be wealth in mid-life and old age.

The 27th Day: They are extravagant and unpredictable, but they will have good health. Their future will be more promising after the age of thirty.

The 28th Day: They will experience both joy and bitterness, with no help from parents. They will have a relatively quality life, though it will be unremarkable.

The 29th Day: They will enjoy sweetness after tasting bitterness. They will have to work hard at young age, but good

The Rat Eating Grapes

This is a motif commonly expressed in Chinese paper-cuts and in New Year pictures. The Rat distinguishes itself amazingly in propagation. As stated in *Compendium of Materia Medica* by Li Shizhen (1518–1593) in 1590, the Rat gives birth to its babies only after a month's pregnancy, sometimes with as many as twenty babies! Such ability of having more children in a short period of time is really longed for by people who want to have more children. Therefore, the Rat represents more children. Grapes are full of seeds and seeds (*zi*) sound like children in Chinese. For this, people put the Rat together with grapes to reinforce their desire for energetic propagation.

luck will come in mid-life. Both the male and the female can benefit from their spouses.

The 30th Day: Smart and lively, they enjoy performing acts of kindness with no worries about future. They will enjoy wealth and prosperity after mid-life, with lots of happiness and a long life ahead.

Overall Fortunes of the Rat Born in Different Hours

11 PM–1 AM: There will be happiness throughout life. Despite the absence of family wealth, they are marked by a firm character, intelligence, deft hands, and the habit of pondering over questions. They are able to become successful in career thanks to the help from others.

1 AM–3 AM: They will experience joy throughout life. They will benefit from lots of help and support from family. In particular, the woman can expect financial support from family members and be comfortable throughout life. The man will find beautiful wife who will have access to wealth. He will have a successful career, though he will lose a great extent of wealth.

3 AM–5 AM: They will experience joy throughout life and live a comfortable life without any worries. The man will be clever, smart, and versatile, with lots of money and wealth in life. The woman will be beautiful and smart with lots of support from family, but she will lose money easily. It will be difficult for the female Rat's career to be as successful as the male Rat's.

5 AM–7 AM: They will enjoy wealth, happiness, peace, and joy throughout life. There will be very much help from family, especially parents. They will receive support at home and help from outside, hence experiencing success quickly. They are bold and intelligent. If they cannot become a person of power, they will become a very rich person instead.

7 AM–9 AM: They will encounter twists and turns as well as rise and fall throughout life. Despite great ambition, talent, and

knowledge, they will not have support from family. Even when they experience success in career at a certain time, they are not able to keep it going.

9 AM–11 AM: With twists and turns in life and a career that is neither outstanding or bad, they will have minimal support from family and others. As a result, it will be hard to have a successful career.

11 AM–1 PM: Their life will be a series of sharp rise and fall and they will experience misfortune and honor throughout life, sometimes both at the same time. Success makes them arrogant and failures make them overly frustrated. They are hot-tempered, which makes it difficult to get along with others.

1 PM–3 PM: Their life will rise and fall like a wave and they will not be able to count on help and support from family or others. Their stubborn nature will help in having a successful career. They should manage the career well, otherwise, it will plunge into a downfall.

3 PM–5 PM: Their life will be marked with good fortune all the time. They are noble in character, and their good qualities and talents, as well as devotion to family and respect of superiors, along with an abundance of help from others, will be factors in growing their career. However, they will encounter many twists and turns and suffer from financial loss several times, but that will not affect the basic course of their life.

5 PM–7 PM: They will enjoy peace throughout life with tremendous help and support from parents. Kind-hearted and righteous, they will also have help from others, ensuring a steady career. However, it will be without many pay offs.

7 PM–9 PM: There will be hardship throughout life. Their parents will be subjected to health concerns, so they will spend time taking care of parents as well as networking with others and pursue career.

9 PM–11 PM: They will have good relationship with parents. Though they will not have major problems in daily life, they will not achieve much career development due to health issues.

Chapter Two
The Ox

The second animal in the Chinese zodiac is the Ox, who represents diligence and stability. Among the twelve signs, the Ox stands in sharp contrast to the Rat as the biggest in size. Therefore, people equate the Rat with the notion of smallness or having less, while the Ox is associated with immensity and having more.

Lunar Years of the Ox in the Solar Calendar

4 February 1913 to 3 February 1914

4 February 1925 to 3 February 1926

4 February 1937 to 3 February 1938

4 February 1949 to 3 February 1950

4 February 1961 to 3 February 1962

4 February 1973 to 3 February 1974

4 February 1985 to 3 February 1986

4 February 1997 to 3 February 1998

3 February 2009 to 3 February 2010

3 February 2021 to 3 February 2022

3 February 2033 to 3 February 2034

3 February 2045 to 2 February 2046

Life Path

People born in the year of the Ox tend to cherish ideals and ambitions. They do things according to their own will and ability, hold strong to their beliefs, and attach great importance to work and family. Experiencing above average luck and opportunities as teenagers, they will leave home to start from scratch at an early age. It is only in mid-life that they will endure hardship, aggravation, and a loss of faith, but happiness will return to them in old age.

Personality

Ox people are mild, honest, patient, diligent, independent, enthusiastic, and firm. At the same time, they can be stubborn and a bit unsociable. Their most obvious merits are marked by a strong sense of responsibility in a down-to-earth manner and thorough consideration before they make a decision on anything. And once they have made a decision, they would courageously carry it out and try to overcome any adversity. Born with a sense of righteousness, Ox people are stubborn, conservative, and faithful to traditions. However, it is beneficial for them to give up their own views and try to be adaptable when face with temporary upheavals.

Profession

Ox people are hardworking and diligent. Their stable characters and a fairly strong ability to deliberate makes them suitable for analytical work and anything related to professional techniques and knowledge, hence enjoying smooth success in their career development. They need to be mindful of envious people who will cause trouble and learn to be adaptable in order to overcome adversity.

Five Oxen

Five Oxen by Han Huang (723–787) is one of the most outstanding animal-themed works in the history of Chinese arts. It is now preserved in the Beijing Palace Museum.

The five oxen in the painting are featured by different images and postures, as well as spirited eyes with profound and vivid expression. Their mild and stubborn characters are perfectly revealed. Viewers can obviously feel their life and sentiments as well as their different inner perceptions. This painting is likely to eulogize important Confucian philosophy in China, i.e. benevolence, righteousness, etiquettes, wisdom and trustworthiness, or solemnity, loyalty, respect, sincerity, and courage. It is very appropriate to compare the noble virtue to the farm ox as a good friend of mankind.

Love and Marriage

Though they have a tendency to be sentimental, the Ox knows whom to love and whom to hate. It is a pity their good luck tends to disappear due to their lack of ability to show themselves and take initiative to connect with other people. In spite of this, their honesty deserves praise. They will be with the right people if they are always honest.

Besides another Ox, they are suited to be matched with those of the Rat, the Snake, and the Rooster. There will be quick disagreements if they are matched with those of the Horse, the

Sheep, the Dragon, and the Dog, hence requiring adjustment for balance and happiness.

Marriage Compatibility with Women Born in Other Animal Years

The Ox Man with the Rat Woman: This a mutually beneficial and satisfying relationship where both will get what they need from each other.

The Ox Man with the Ox Woman: While both are very diligent they are not outgoing and energetic enough, hence lacking a lighthearted joyfulness in their life together.

The Ox Man with the Tiger Woman: With few things in common, they come together probably due to curiosity but fail to truly understand each other in the end.

The Ox Man with the Rabbit Woman: Communication and compromise are constantly needed to bring satisfaction to their marriage.

The Ox Man with the Dragon Woman: Since both of them are marked by a decisive personality and stubbornness, there will be constant clashes. The best way to keep the relationship going is to look at the spouse with admiration and communicate with sweet words.

The Ox Man with the Snake Woman: This is a truly perfect marriage.

The Ox Man with the Horse Woman: It is difficult to coordinate between them.

The Ox Man with the Sheep Woman: Their relationship will

be full of disagreements, sadness, joy, separation, and reunion, yet they will lasts forever.

The Ox Man with the Monkey Woman: Due to their inadequately tacit understanding, neither of them can convince the other.

The Ox Man with the Rooster Woman: This will be a happy marriage.

The Ox Man with the Dog Woman: This will not be a happy match, with the root of it attributed to the difference in personalities.

The Ox Man with the Pig Woman: This is a perfect match, which benefits from their nice characters.

Marriage Compatibility with Men Born in Other Animal Years

The Ox Woman with the Rat Man: This will be a very happy match and the couple will be universally admired.

The Ox Woman with the Ox Man: Both of them are very diligent but not outgoing enough; their relationship will lack flexibility.

The Ox Woman with the Tiger Man: Their personalities run counter to each other and stubbornness is almost the only common characteristic they will share.

The Ox Woman with the Rabbit Man: It will take time for them to adapt to each other.

The Ox Woman with the Dragon Man: Both of them are stubborn, so they will have to come to mutual compromise.

The Ox Woman with the Snake Man: They will share each other's ups and downs. Their marriage will be tender and sweet.

The Ox Woman with the Horse Man: They have completely different characters, lacking common interests and habits.

The Ox Woman with the Sheep Man: Efforts from both sides are required to make fairly big changes, but their marriage will likely end up to be a desirable one.

The Ox Woman with the Monkey Man: Both are outstanding but very stubborn individuals, often refusing to compromise

The Herd-Boy and the Weaving Girl

This noted folk legend in China originates from the worship of ancient people for stars, i.e. the outcome of deifying and personalizing stars.

As the legend goes, since parents of the herd-boy died early, he was only accompanied by an old ox. The weaving girl is said to be the granddaughter of the Emperor of Heaven and the Queen Mother. The weaving girl often came down to the human world together with her sisters and took a bath in the river. The old ox hinted at the poor and helpless herd-boy to steal the clothes of the weaving girl, compelling the weaving girl to stay behind in the human world and marry the herd-boy. After marriage, the husband went farming while the wife engaged in weaving, having children and living a happy life.

Upon hearing this, the Queen Mother flew into a rage and tried all she could to get the weaving girl back. Consequently, the couple had to meet by the Milky Way only on the seventh day of the seventh lunar month every year, with magpies building up a bridge to help them get across the Milky Way for a meeting. This is how the seventh day of the seventh lunar month has become the Valentine's Day in China.

with each other.

The Ox Woman with the Rooster Man: Their marriage will last forever, even becoming an example for others.

The Ox Woman with the Dog Man: Both take marriage seriously, but they need to compromise with each other.

The Ox Woman with the Pig Man: They truly love each other, but it will take time for them to adapt to each other.

The Luck of Wealth

People born in the Ox year are diligent and courageous with relatively modest wealth. Because of their lack of personal financial acumen, they will not enjoy great wealth, but instead enjoy a stable life with a decent amount in savings.

Overall Fortunes of the Ox in Different Animal Years

The Year of the Rat: Everything is smooth sailing. Intuitive foresight will bring about beneficial opportunities from bad luck each time. Small health problems will naturally be cured without taking medicine.

The Year of the Ox: Their luck tends to be average without fame and wealth. However, they can gain these things if they work meticulously.

The Year of the Tiger: There will be a lack of external resistance so they will experience beneficial opportunities. Someone in their family will get married. By the end of the year, efforts will often be in vain as it will only yield little above average results.

The Year of the Rabbit: Adversity will be experienced often. Everything will be fine if they behave tolerantly. They will enjoy peace year round if they strive to keep a balance state of mind.

The Year of the Dragon: If they follow the law of nature to

retreat in order to advance, they will not have much to worry about in their daily life.

The Year of the Snake: They will enjoy great wealth. However, those born in the odd months do not have the luck to enjoy the great wealth. Those born in the even months will know to take action at the right time. There will be frequent disputes regarding what is right and wrong.

The Year of the Horse: They should be mindful of losing their wealth. Lost wealth can be regained thanks to the help of benefactors at the end of the year.

The Year of the Sheep: They will be in an unfavorable situation at the beginning of the year but there is light at the end of the tunnel, so to speak. They will experience good luck at the end of the year.

The Year of the Monkey: They will have very good luck and almost every effort results in beneficial gains, such as passing an exam, entering into a happy marriage, or the birth of a child. However, they should strive for contentment instead of extreme highs and lows.

The Year of Rooster: There will be more external resistance and not as many opportunities. They will enjoy peace if they do more good things for others.

The Year of the Dog: There will be less external resistance and more opportunities. Their career will be smooth sailing, but they should be meticulous in their planning.

The Year of the Pig: There will be obstacles so things will be hard to be accomplished. But they will have help from benefactors at the end of the year. They will have savings as long as they are diligent and thrifty.

Overall Fortunes of the Ox Born in Different Months by the Lunar Calendar

The 1st Lunar Month: Good luck will be scarce in the early years, opportunities come in middle age, and happiness and longevity will be enjoyed in old age. Self-reliance will yield prosperity.

与下双驹大秦牛 今年日子不用愁六畜兴旺五谷丰收

牛 春

Whipping the Ox in Spring

As folk customs in ancient times, on the day when spring began according to the Chinese lunar calendar, people disguised themselves as spring deities in charge of the growth of grass and trees, whipping the Ox as a ceremony of greeting the advent of spring. Since spring is the farming season, worshipping spring deities and matching it with the Ox symbolic of farming demonstrate the importance of spring farming.

This painting is a representative of Wuqiang's New Year Painting (Wuqiang County, Hebei Province) which is Chinese folk art developed under the influence of primitive farming, Buddhist ideas, traditional concepts and national habits. They are marked by full structure, bold lines, bright colors, exaggerated decoration, and strong festive characteristics.

The 2nd Lunar Month: Courageous actions done with the desire for amazing career achievements will have counter-productive results.

The 3rd Lunar Month: Very smart and knowledgeable, and without much effort, they will enjoy a pleasant and worry-free life. When they are away from home, respect will be earned.

The 4th Lunar Month: Without the ability to hold a high position in society, opportunities and wealth will be average.

The 5th Lunar Month: Though kind-hearted and devoted to parents, the lack of help from influential people will hamper the ability to make much money.

The 6th Lunar Month: With outstanding intelligence, working hard in the early years will gradually lead to prosperity after middle age. Benefactors will help them. There will be less external resistance and more good luck.

The 7th Lunar Month: Smart and intelligent, a wealthy life will be enjoyed with no serious disasters or illnesses. Old age will be a long and happy one.

The 8th Lunar Month: Being healthy, smart, and flexible, they will enjoy both wealth and fame.

The 9th Lunar Month: Blessed with intelligence and a good work ethic, along with courage and intuition, notice and help from benefactors, they will have an outstanding career and supremely full life.

The 10th Lunar Month: Early years will be in poverty, but prosperity will come in youth or middle age. Smart and resolute, achievements will be noticed. Wealth will be enjoyed as a result of extremely clever business acumen.

The 11th Lunar Month: Setbacks will be encountered often without much help from benefactors.

The 12th Lunar Month: Despite enjoying a great family life and having great ambitions and energy, fame will always be achieved without much wealth.

Overall Fortunes of the Ox Born on Different Days by the Lunar Calendar

The 1st Day: Clever, smart, and sincere, they will work hard in early years and enjoy happiness in old age. The women Ox are hardworking and good at handling family affairs.

The 2nd Day: They are well respected by people and will enjoy a smooth life in middle age and old age without much worries. They are kind-hearted, so life will be benevolent and reward them with longevity.

The 3rd Day: Smart, clever, and enterprising with outstanding talents, they will enjoy many kinds of happiness. Luck will be average in early years, but success and wealth will come after middle age.

The 4th Day: Though they possess outstanding characteristics, their luck will be up and down. The woman Ox is luckier than the man.

The 5th Day: Being of weak-willed, they learn more but accomplish less. With average luck in early years, they will become prosperous thanks to help from benefactors. They will also enjoy stability and longevity.

The 6th Day: Innately smart, they do things in a stable and meticulous way, so they will accomplish a lot. Talented and intelligent, they will work hard when they are young, experience a turning point in luck in middle age, and enjoy stability in old age.

The 7th Day: Courteous and eager to learn, they have outstanding talents and intelligence. While they experience hardship as a teenager, they become successful in career in middle age and enjoy a happy married and family life.

The 8th Day: There will be many twists and turns in early years, but there will be help from influential people after they are thirty years old, resulting in prosperity.

The 9th Day: They are kind-hearted and get on well with others. The man Ox is handsome while the woman is smart and pretty.

The 10th Day: They will enjoy a full career and a happy family. With average luck in early years, they will become wealthy in middle and old age.

The 11th Day: They are resolute in handling things and courageous in what they do. However, they will not be very rich, but instead will live a life of moderate wealth.

The 12th Day: They are mild and able to bear hardship. Despite twists and turns in teenage years, they will be prosperous in middle age, enjoying both happiness and wealth.

The 13th Day: Born into wealth and happiness, they are respected by people. They will have many benefactors, hence enjoying a successful and comfortable life.

The 14th Day: The man Ox is honest, tranquil, composed, and handsome, while the woman is smart. Both have average luck in the early years, but enjoy happiness after middle age.

The 15th Day: Both the man and woman Ox will enjoy a very desirable married life.

The 16th Day: They are smart with outstanding skills. However, they have no access to family wealth. Despite not much hard work, they are not so relaxed. They will only enjoy sweetness after tasting bitterness, so happiness will come later in life.

The 17th Day: Being patient, they will have average luck in early years, but enjoy accomplishments later.

The 18th Day: Being highly intuitive, they disregard others, and take pride in their intelligence. The woman Ox, who is luckier than the man, is benevolent and get on well with others, hence enjoying happiness and longevity.

The 19th Day: With fame and the wealth that comes with it, they will enjoy prosperity in middle age and a comfortable life in old age.

The 20th Day: They work hard, but suffer from much vexation. They will gain more wealth if they work away from home and enjoy happiness in old age.

The 21st Day: Both the man and woman Ox will have nice spouses. Being versatile, they are fond of speculation and disregard others. They need to focus more, otherwise they may not enjoy happiness in old age.

The 22nd Day: Both the man and woman Ox are clever and smart. They abide by promise, do things in a down-to-earth manner, and maintain good relationships with others. They will

The Ox-Head and Deer-Antler Gold Dangling Hairpin (*Bu Yao*)

Length: 19.4 cm. Weight: 87.37 g.

Hair Decoration in Northern Dynasty (386–581)

National Museum of China

According to the folk legend, the Ox stands for wealth since it is concerned with the harvest thanks to its hard work in farming. The ox head and ox horn of this hairpin are clearly outlined in vivid and attractive appearance. A branch of the deer-antler shape is seen amidst two ox horns and each branch tip is hung with a gold leaf of the peach shape. There are fourteen gold leaves in total, each can tremble when it is waved.

During the period of the Wei Dynasty (220–265), the Jin Dynasty (265–420), and the Northern and Southern Dynasties (420–589), this was a head-decoration for women. Gold leaves would tremble when the woman's head waved while walking. This gold decoration was not only a fashion, but also the symbol of the social position at that time.

enjoy sweetness after tasting bitterness and live a very prosperous life in old age.

The 23rd Day: They will often change professions and residences. The woman Ox, who is luckier than the man, lives a more carefree life.

The 24th Day: Good luck will be tempered with bad luck. There will be happiness and wealth if they are born on an hour with a lucky trend. If not, they will experience an average life of worries and burdens.

The 25th Day: The man Ox will have a nice wife, knows the ways of business, and will enjoy a full career. The woman Ox is kind-hearted, get on well with others, and handles family affairs ingeniously. She is bound to be happy later.

The 26th Day: Lively, optimistic, and light-hearted, they sacrifice for the sake of others. They will enjoy a promising future thanks to good luck, and will be blessed with devoted children.

The 27th Day: The man Ox deserves praise for his honesty. He works hard, is bold, unrestrained, and generous, thus will enjoy wealth and have a nice spouse. The woman Ox is smart and pretty, enjoying a carefree life.

The 28th Day: The man Ox will suffer from bad luck first before enjoying good luck, while the woman is luckier, but lives an average life.

The 29th Day: They will often change residences and professions. They can gain wealth easily with a promising future if they stay away from home for career.

The 30th Day: Kind-hearted, they act decently both in private and public. They are respected and admired by people, enjoying sweetness after tasting bitterness.

Overall Fortunes of the Ox Born in Different Hours

11 PM–1 AM: Their family will enjoy prosperity and they will have a carefree life in old age. Their health will be average.

1 AM–3 AM: They are smart, knowledgeable and talented, with outstanding writing capacity. However, they lack help from others and cannot accomplish what they desire.

3 AM–5 AM: Not being very social, they don't like to work with others and tend to fail in doing things. However, they will have help from others, so there will not be many serious problems in life.

5 AM–7 AM: Without much help from others, they will suffer from many twists and turns in life. However, they are firm and persistent.

7 AM–9 AM: Not having much luck, they often encounter obstacles in doing things. Despite living a comfortable life, they will never have a lot in savings.

9 AM–11 AM: Having a desirable title, happiness, and wealth, they will enjoy a very comfortable life, but they will encounter many jealous people.

11 AM–1 PM: Both the man and the woman Ox should be mindful when dealing with marriage.

1 PM–3 PM: Even with quite a lot of twists and turns in life, both the man and woman Ox will have supportive spouses.

3 PM–5 PM: They enjoy unbelievable happiness and wealth—even bad luck will turn to good luck. They will be helped by influential people in work and career.

5 PM–7 PM: They will suffer from lots of twists and turns in life and will lose money and wealth without reason.

7 PM–9 PM: They will be far away from home while engaged in a great career. Open-minded and outgoing, they enjoy great wealth and meet helpful people wherever they go. They never worry about life and are always successful in what they do. However, they should be mindful of struggling with others.

9 PM–11 PM: They will be far away from home while engaging in a great career, but they are indifferent to other family members.

Chapter Three
The Tiger

For many people, the Tiger is power. People born in the year of the Tiger speak and act in a supremely royal manner. Therefore, the tiger, who ranks third in the Chinese zodiac, represents majesty and fierceness.

Lunar Years of the Tiger in the Solar Calendar

4 February 1914 to 4 February 1915

4 February 1926 to 4 February 1927

4 February 1938 to 4 February 1939

4 February 1950 to 3 February 1951

4 February 1962 to 3 February 1963

4 February 1974 to 3 February 1975

4 February 1986 to 3 February 1987

4 February 1998 to 3 February 1999

4 February 2010 to 3 February 2011

4 February 2022 to 3 February 2023

4 February 2034 to 3 February 2035

3 February 2046 to 3 February 2047

Life Path

People born in the year of the Tiger look lenient and benevolent, but are firm and powerful in their personality. They will rise and fall in life. With the advent of good luck in early years, their luck in middle age is marked by uncertainty. For a time, they enjoy good opportunities after middle age, and some of them will also have high prestige in old age. Throughout life, their peace and health lie in moving around. Particular mention should be made that Tiger people are strongly independent while they outweigh others in terms of will power and risky spirit. They are apt to lack the spirit of coordination and cooperation as well as have enemies. Therefore, they should try to avoid being dictators.

Personality

Tiger people are ambitious and fully confident about themselves. Innately fond of taking challenges, they are masculine, enthusiastic, and courageous. The more frustrated they are, the fiercer they are. They never give up until things are done. They dislike obeying others and enjoy bringing others under their control. Their frank and above-board personality makes it easy for them to win trust.

However, what should be avoided is that they don't have close friends despite their extensive contacts with others since they are fond of being on their own. Their innate stubbornness also makes them anti-social among people.

Profession

Tiger people look majestic without showing anger. With great self-confidence, they are characterized as leaders. They are most interested in guiding others or exerting management over the public. Instead of following the logical order, they are active in posing questions or plans, always pressing for improvement. If asked to do the same job at a fixed place for a long time, they need to be provided with a space of innovative thinking so as to give play to their strong points.

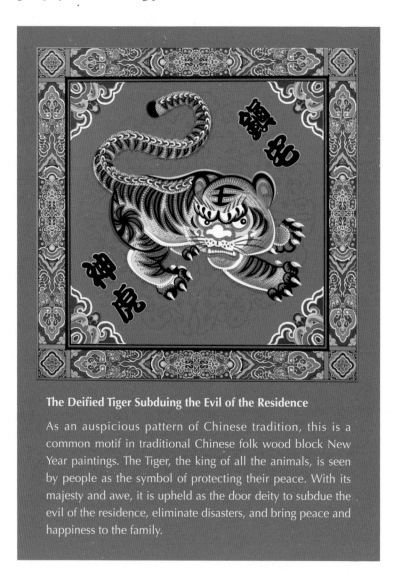

The Deified Tiger Subduing the Evil of the Residence

As an auspicious pattern of Chinese tradition, this is a common motif in traditional Chinese folk wood block New Year paintings. The Tiger, the king of all the animals, is seen by people as the symbol of protecting their peace. With its majesty and awe, it is upheld as the door deity to subdue the evil of the residence, eliminate disasters, and bring peace and happiness to the family.

Love and Marriage

Tiger people are as fierce as the tiger in dealing with love. Innately kind-hearted, they know how to please their spouse and they don't care about being generous to others, hence being particularly favored by their spouse. However, they want to see their spouse do all things according to their way. Therefore, they need to be careful not to be capricious in their contacts with others. Instead, they should be frank and honest, paying great attention to maintaining relations with others. It is suitable for Tiger people to be matched with those born in the year of the Horse, the Dog and the Pig. They should be careful with those of the Monkey and the Snake.

Marriage Compatibility with Women Born in Other Animal Years

The Tiger Man with the Rat Woman: They can live together, but the Rat woman must be lenient because the Tiger man likes to take risks occasionally.

The Tiger Man with the Ox Woman: They are both marked by stubbornness. Therefore, they need to double their efforts to compromise for the sake of living together.

The Tiger Man with the Tiger Woman: There will be some obstacles in their marriage because they are both unrealistic, hence leading to instability when starting their family.

The Tiger Man with the Rabbit Woman: This is a fairly good match. Despite possible quarrels, they understand each other and the Rabbit woman knows how to be a supportive wife and a nurturing mother.

The Tiger Man with the Dragon Woman: This is a happy marriage. Both of them have firm characters and are mutually supportive of each other. The Dragon woman in particular is very helpful to the Tiger man in his career.

The Tiger Man with the Snake Woman: Both need to reinforce mutual understanding. Otherwise, it is difficult to have a happy family life.

The Tiger Man with the Horse Woman: This is a fairly happy marriage. Their children are devoted to them.

The Tiger Man with the Sheep Woman: Both need to avoid misunderstanding and quarrels which will lead to the loss of love due to anger.

The Tiger Man with the Monkey Woman: Conflicts break out easily between them, particularly in terms of money and property.

The Tiger Man with the Rooster Woman: This is a good match and the marriage can last forever.

The Tiger Man with the Dog Woman: They can live well together and support each other.

The Tiger Man with the Pig Woman: They can live together. Though the Tiger man is offensive to some extent, making the Pig woman feel uncomfortable, the latter knows and admires the former and has ample patience to take care of him.

Marriage Compatibility with Men Born in Other Animal Years

The Tiger Woman with the Rat Man: The Tiger woman is a dreamer, making it difficult for the Rat man to meet her needs, hence resulting in problems.

The Tiger Woman with the Ox Man: For a happy marriage, the Ox man cannot always think about controlling the Tiger woman.

The Tiger Woman with the Tiger Man: Wisdom is needed for them to live together.

The Tiger Woman with the Rabbit Man: Both need to exert great efforts to bring about a happy marriage, because the Tiger woman has a complex personality while the Rabbit man is considerably fragile.

The Tiger Woman with the Dragon Man: This is a happy marriage, but there may be setbacks. However, the Dragon man understands the Tiger woman, with the latter being willing to accept the advice of the former.

The Tiger Woman with the Snake Man: They have different aspirations and interests and find it difficult to communicate with each other.

The Tiger Woman with the Horse Man: This is a great match, with happiness throughout their life together.

The Tiger Woman with the Sheep Man: Their marriage is marked by problems and monotony.

The Tiger Woman with the Monkey Man: They are too particular about each other, far from being a great match.

The Tiger Woman with the Rooster Man: They will lead a colorful life together, yet will also be tested at the same time.

The Tiger Woman with the Dog Man: They can live together, but sometimes find themselves distracted, because both of them are fond of illusions that are far removed from real life.

The Tiger Woman with the Pig Man: They can live well together, as long as the Tiger woman does not unconsciously harm and take advantage of the kindness of the Pig man.

The Luck of Wealth

The biggest belief of people born in the year of the Tiger is not money, but something more spiritual. Therefore, they generally do not care or worry about where their money comes from, since they have many economic sources. Their wealth tends to be dependent on the ideal and objective that they pursue. An appropriate objective will naturally bring them wealth.

They are generous and optimistic, paying less attention to money. Despite a handsome amount of income, their wealth comes and goes easily. Therefore, they should give play to their ability of financing, focus on the planning of being economical, and adjust their investment plan with a definitive objective.

Overall Fortunes of the Tiger in Different Animal Years

The Year of the Rat: There are more unfavorable situations than favorable ones. Therefore, Tiger people should stay at home more, devote themselves to their own undertakings, and do more things in a down-to-earth manner.

The Year of the Ox: As a year of immense potential, there is good luck falling upon Tiger people. They should lose no time in seizing opportunities. At the beginning of the year, they need to be more careful.

The Year of the Tiger: Because of instability, Tiger people in this year often feel dissatisfactory in doing things.

The Year of the Rabbit: As an auspicious year, Tiger people in this year can do as much as possible. However, they should not be carried away by their good luck. Instead, they should do more kind deeds.

The Year of the Dragon: There are more bad luck and less opportunities, along with sharp ups and downs, hence making it difficult to do all things well. Tiger people should adhere to their own undertakings and advance cautiously in order to be peaceful throughout the year.

The Year of the Snake: There are more expenses without progress. However, there still exist favorable situations, and emphatic efforts for progress can lead to success.

The Year of the Horse: Everything is smooth sailing. However, they should be mindful of going to extremes and guard against people with ulterior motives.

The Year of the Sheep: It does not matter much despite small consumption of wealth and minor illness. Tiger people in this year should exert restraint for stability, try to make more good friends and less enemies.

The Year of the Monkey: It is difficult to accomplish anything.

The Year of the Rooster: All bad luck can be turned into opportunities. However, Tiger people in this year should avoid going too far in their efforts to be successful.

The Year of the Dog: Everything is smooth sailing. There will be no worries once health is taken good care of.

The Year of the Pig: Destiny-oriented trends recede, along with obvious ups and downs. Therefore, Tiger people in this year should be plan well in advance as well as be careful in doing things.

Tiger-Head Shoes

As one of traditional Chinese arts and crafts, they are child shoes with toe caps of tiger head patterns. In addition, there are tiger-shaped caps, tiger-shaped pillows and tiger-shaped cloth figurines. They are of practical and appreciative value while serving as auspicious objects. People endow them with the function of warding off ghosts and evils, believing that they can protect children and pray for smooth growth of children with them.

Overall Fortunes of the Tiger Born in Different Months by the Lunar Calendar

The 1st Lunar Month: People born in this month are pure and possess an upright personality, firm character, and will achieve fame and wealth.

The 2nd Lunar Month: People born in this month are faithful and devoted to their parents. They possess intelligence and ability.

They will receive respect by everyone outside the home as well as serve as models in their own home.

The 3rd Lunar Month: People born in this month are in a quite unfavorable situation in their early years, but find themselves on the path of rapid career development in the youth or middle age. Whatever they do, they would make desirable achievements out of the expectation of other people.

The 4th Lunar Month: People born in this month enjoy smooth sailing in everything they do. They will have wealth and live leisurely throughout their life without much worries.

The 5th Lunar Month: Starting from scratch, people born in this month are very courageous, well educated, but also hot-tempered. They are able to be successful in their undertakings to the extent of being very powerful. However, they often step on the toes of others and quarrel with them.

The 6th Lunar Month: People born in this month experience more twists and turns, almost without opportunities of becoming successful. Despite great ambitions, they do not have help from others, hence making it difficult to accomplish their goals.

The 7th Lunar Month: People born in this month are marked by a firm character and extraordinary energy. However, they are poorly grounded in their family background, leading a hard life in their early years. After middle age, they will distinguish themselves with outstanding career development.

The 8th Lunar Month: People born in this month are innately bright, unusually intelligent, and incomparably outstanding when it comes to education. They are able to perceive things in advance, hence enjoying admiration throughout their life.

The 9th Lunar Month: People born in this month are bookworms and are conceited and impractical. Seldom helped by others, they will come across setbacks from time to time.

The 10th Lunar Month: People born in this month are characterized by intelligence, focus on the codes of brotherhood, and have a mild personality and elegant behavior. However, they work hard throughout their life without much accomplishments.

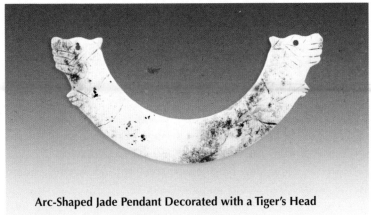

Arc-Shaped Jade Pendant Decorated with a Tiger's Head

Length: 11.9 cm. Width: 1.9 cm. Thickness: 0.5 cm. Color: grey/
white with some yellow stains.
Ornamental jade from the Neolithic Lingjiatan culture
Lingjiatan Site, Hanshang, Anhui Province, Tomb No. 8
Anhui Institute of Cultural Relics and Archaeology

This piece is the earliest known arc-shaped pendant. Flat
and arc-shaped, both ends are decorated with tiger heads in
relief with eyes, nose and ears as well as the wrinkled head
and forward facing claws incised or drilled out. Incisions
on the pendant represent the tiger's stripes. The pendant is
unique in form. Four other tiger head arc-shaped pendants
were excavated at Lingjiatan, demonstrating the reverence in
which tigers were held.

The 11th Lunar Month: People born in this month work
hard throughout their life. They enjoy a carefree life despite little
career accomplishments.

The 12th Lunar Month: People born in this month are apt
to encounter those with ulterior motives. They do not have help
from others and come across setbacks from time to time. They
should be careful and cautious, trying to unite with colleagues
and make more friends so as to be more successful in their
career.

Overall Fortunes of the Tiger Born on Different Days by the Lunar Calendar

The 1st Day: They are characterized by innate intelligence and energy. Their luck is just average in early years, but outstanding in middle age.

The 2nd Day: They enjoy good luck in early years, along with leisure and joy. Their luck is just average in middle age. They get on well with others with help from influential people.

The 3rd Day: They have talent, wisdom, intelligence, sound virtue, and a happy family and marriage.

The 4th Day: They will all have supportive spouses, but need to take care of their own health and the health of their spouses.

The 5th Day: With kind hearts, integrity, and an ordinary family background, they leave home for work with promising futures.

The 6th Day: Leading a hard life in early years with no relatives to rely on, they paddle their own canoes and work hard, enjoying sweet success after trying bitterness. They have good health.

The 7th Day: The Tiger man born on this day enjoys both happiness and wealth. Their luck is just average in early years, but outstanding in the middle age. They will make success.

The 8th Day: Despite possessing intelligence, they are weak-willed with the lack of intuition and the absence of good luck. They can accomplish nothing unless they are helped by others.

The 9th Day: They are fond of being economical and hardworking, with more hard work as their fate. Despite just average luck in early years, they live quite comfortably in old age.

The 10th Day: Coming across more helpful people than ones with ulterior motives in their life, they find it easy to accomplish things and have an ideal family life and career.

The 11th Day: The Tiger man is handsome while the woman is pretty. They are sincere, honest, elegant, and nice. Despite just average luck in early years, they enjoy good luck and wealth in middle age.

The 12th Day: It is better for the Tiger man born on this day to make a fortune by leaving home. The woman born on this day comes across lots of hardship and worries, but gradually embarks on a smooth sailing journey after middle age.

The 13th Day: They are characterized by innate intelligence and obvious artistic talents, with fame and wealth.

The 14th Day: With undesirable luck, obstacles, and difficulties in early years, they work hard and start from scratch. With sweetness coming after bitterness, they live quite comfortably in old age.

The 15th Day: They are quite intelligent, but hot-tempered, capricious, and stubborn. They have difficult relationships with their father and brothers.

The 16th Day: With both fame and wealth, they enjoy an exciting life.

The 17th Day: With both bad luck and opportunities, they lead an unstable life.

The 18th Day: With a blessed marriage, they enjoy happiness in old age though not much progress is made before middle age.

The 19th Day: With innate intelligence, they value trustworthiness and do things in a down-to-earth manner. The first half of their life is just average, but the second half is expected to enjoy wealth.

The 20th Day: Sincere and honest, they are fond of doing kind deeds. They endure hardship in early years, with some unavoidable small tragedies.

The 21st Day: With all things to their satisfaction in childhood, they experience lots of ups and downs as well as hardship in their youth and start from the bottom in their career.

The 22nd Day: Weak-willed and uncertain in doing things, they often change their jobs and residences. They have a hard time in childhood and enjoy good luck in middle age.

The 23rd Day: Intelligent and kind-hearted, they hold power and have considerable wealth.

The 24th Day: With a smooth sailing journey coming after bitterness, they are expected to be successful after middle age with both fame and wealth.

The 25th Day: They enjoy a smooth sailing journey after some hardship.

The 26th Day: They suffer from tragedies in childhood and lead an ordinary life in their youth, with no friends and relatives to rely on.

The 27th Day: They are destined to have supreme opportunities, to be promoted, and enjoy ways leading to good luck, a happy marriage, and many children.

The 28th Day: With a firm personality, less wisdom, and ample courage, they often come across problems in addition to indifferent relations with family members.

The 29th Day: With an ordinary family background, they make success after leaving home thanks to help from others who bring infinite opportunities for their future. Leading an ordinary life in early years, they enjoy good luck and family prosperity in middle and old age.

The 30th Day: They have their own business, though they will be without many children.

Overall Fortunes of the Tiger Born in Different Hours

11 PM–1 AM: With many trouble and ups and downs throughout life, they have high aspirations but less talents, hence working hard without success.

1 AM–3 AM: Having joy throughout life, they are always assisted by people who help them turn bad luck into opportunities and make all things successful. Intelligent, quick-witted, broad-minded, and lenient, they don't care about things against their satisfaction and even find them amusing. Tiger people born in this period are slightly unhealthy.

3 AM–5 AM: Intelligent, smart and flexible, they are characterized by amazing memory and highly educated, hence enjoying respect throughout their life. However, they lead a hard

life in their early years with no help from relatives. They develop their career completely from their own efforts.

5 AM–7 AM: Romantic and spruce, they have no interest in making progress. They're gifted with a nice appearance and cleverness, but make no practical value out of it.

7 AM–9 AM: Despite working hard throughout life, they seldom have the luck of success. However, they are intelligent, quick-witted, and well educated. Many tragedies do not affect them much. They can accomplish outstandingly unless they leave home. They enjoy good health and seldom suffer from illness.

9 AM–11 AM: They go through many ups and downs, with few opportunities for success. They are poorly grounded in their family background and don't have a close relationship with their brothers. However, there is profound love in their marriage. They are narrow-minded, gloomy all day long, and very particular about trifles.

11 AM–1 PM: Fair and dignify with outstanding courage and talents, they are the elites in society, giving their life-long contributions, hence being respected by all. They are devoted so much to parents and immensely affectionate with their spouses.

1 PM–3 PM: With bad luck that are invariably turned into opportunities, they live a comfortable life and enjoy every success since they are often helped by others. However, they hardly get help from their parents, hence resorting to their own efforts for career development.

3 PM–5 PM: They are supposed to leave home for career development. Faithful and honest, they never harbor any evil intention at other people. They work in defiance of hardship and danger, hence enjoying appreciation from their superior, getting promoted and becoming noticeable examples. Despite injury in the course of giving service, they don't have to worry about it since it can only make their future more brilliant.

5 PM–7 PM: Destined to be lucky, they are smart, highly efficient, intelligent, and flexible. If born in the right month, they will surely become the elites in society as well as receive profound respect and love. However, they suffer from minor

illness and many ups and downs throughout life. With the help of others, their bad luck are always turned into opportunities.

7 PM–9 PM: Leading a hard life of poverty in their youth, they are intelligent and smart with unique talents, in addition to a particularly strong adaptability and the ability of verbal expression. They become gradually prosperous after middle age and well educated.

9 PM–11 PM: Despite their talents, they are seldom helped by others. Therefore, they have to work hard by relying on themselves, which makes it difficult for them to be successful. After middle age, they can be successful in their own career, but the success cannot last long. They are slightly unhealthy, probably due to the failure to make their aspiration come true.

Chapter Four
The Rabbit

The rabbit has always been regarded as an auspicious animal in China. An example is the story *The Jade-Rabbit in the Moon Palace* that have lasted for several thousand years, with the rabbit being the soul of the bright moon. Therefore, the Rabbit, ranking fourth in the Chinese zodiac, represents tenderness.

Lunar Years of the Rabbit in the Solar Calendar

5 February 1915 to 4 February 1916

5 February 1927 to 4 February 1928

5 February 1939 to 4 February 1940

4 February 1951 to 4 February 1952

4 February 1963 to 4 February 1964

4 February 1975 to 3 February 1976

4 February 1987 to 3 February 1988

4 February 1999 to 3 February 2000

4 February 2011 to 3 February 2012

4 February 2023 to 3 February 2024

4 February 2035 to 3 February 2036

4 February 2047 to 3 February 2048

Life Path

Cherishing sympathy and benevolence, people born in the Rabbit year tend to focus on friendship. There are no obvious ups and downs in the destiny-oriented trends of their life. They seek for progress in a state of stability, reach their career peak in the middle age, and enjoy a smooth sailing journey for the rest of their life.

If they can face difficulties and try to learn from experience, most of them will naturally be successful in their career in middle age.

Personality

They are delicate, acute, innately good-tempered, quiet, optimistic, joyful, enthusiastic about life, courteous, and thoughtful. They are typically favored by everyone. Disliking to be restrained in life, they advance by pursuing ideals and forge ahead with new fashions. However, they find it difficult to be successful due to a weakness in the ability for implementation. They should be careful of being carried away by sentimentality while trying to be open-minded.

Profession

They are characterized by an acute sense of art. Any job related to literature, fine arts, architecture, and music is suitable for them. They are also able to do jobs which require meticulousness and detailed observation. They are good at socializing with others as an advantage, making it suitable for them to handle public relations.

Love and Marriage

They seem to be very fragile, hence making it easy for them to suffer from sentimental contradiction. They should be mindful of the third person who gets involved in their marriage. They need to be cautious when dating someone for the first time, in order to avoid making mistakes and being cheated. It is suitable for them to match with those of the Sheep, the Pig, the Dog, and the Rabbit, and they should be particularly careful when being matched with those of the Rat, the Rooster, the Dragon, and the Ox.

Marriage Compatibility with Women Born in Other Animal Years

The Rabbit Man with the Rat Woman: This is not a good match. The Rabbit man is sociable and often neglects the family and spouse, hence being likely to threaten the position of the Rat woman.

The Rabbit Man with the Ox Woman: The husband should be ready to follow the arrangement of the wife, hence leading to a family life with tacit agreement.

The Rabbit Man with the Tiger Woman: This is not a good marriage, because the Tiger woman is characterized by a complex mentality while the Rabbit man is rather fragile, hence resulting in problems in years to come.

The Rabbit Man with the Rabbit Woman: This is quite an ideal marriage, but both of them must give up naive ideas.

The Rabbit Man with the Dragon Woman: The marriage is an average one, but the Dragon wife should make some sacrifices and must stay at home while trying to keep boredom at bay.

The Rabbit Man with the Snake Woman: The marriage is an average one, but there may be displeasure since both sides are fond of meditation, hence requiring more cautiousness.

The Rabbit Man with the Horse Woman: The existence of love is mainly controlled by the Horse woman. However, even if love fails, the Rabbit man still remains as a loyal friend of the

Jade Pendant in the Form of a Rabbit

Length: 10 cm. Width: 5.8 cm. Thickness: 0.5 cm. Color: yellow / brown.
Ornamental jade in the Late Shang Dynasty (1600–1046 BC)
Tomb of Fu Hao, Anyang, Henan Province
Institute of Archaeology under Chinese Academy of Social Science

Jade rabbits were first seen in the Shang period (1600–1046 BC) and were quite common in the Shang and Zhou periods (1046–256 BC). This piece is flat, representing a rabbit running. The head is slightly raised with two round eyes, open mouth, and protruding tongue. The nose is carved in outline and the ears are laid back. There is a fat, stumpy tail and the feet are thrust forward with the claws and toenails showing. There is a hole drilled through the foot.

Horse woman.

The Rabbit Man with the Sheep Woman: This is a perfect marriage. The Rabbit man is deeply attracted to the rich imagination of the Sheep woman. In addition, their shared artistic talent and temperament serve to further their affections.

The Rabbit Man with the Monkey Woman: Their life is interesting and meaningful. They often like to make fun of others together due to their shared optimistic mentality. However, they should take care not go too far.

The Rabbit Man with the Rooster Woman: For a lasting marriage, the Rabbit man living in the home with the Rooster woman should be free from depression.

The Rabbit Man with the Dog Woman: This is a perfect marriage. The Rabbit man is happy to be with the Dog woman because of her honesty, and the Rabbit man makes up for the shortcomings of the Dog woman.

The Rabbit Man with the Pig Woman: This is quite a happy marriage. Of course, this is because the Pig woman is satisfied with an average and comfortable life.

Marriage Compatibility with Men Born in Other Animal Years

The Rabbit Woman with the Rat Man: Their life is not happy, since the Rabbit woman always does something harmful to the Rat man who refuses to make concession, hence leading to many problems.

The Rabbit Woman with the Ox Man: As long as the Rabbit woman can bear to make concession to the Ox husband, their life will be all right.

The Rabbit Woman with the Tiger Man: There may be displeasure, but both sides understands each other and the Rabbit woman knows how to take care of the husband, hence resulting in a fairly happy marriage.

The Rabbit Woman with the Rabbit Man: This will be a fairly happy marriage as long as both are mature in their ways of thinking.

The Rabbit Woman with the Dragon Man: The Rabbit woman is bright and very sociable, hence being very helpful to the career development of the Dragon husband.

The Rabbit Woman with the Snake Man: They will have an average marriage. It will be better if the Rabbit woman can restrain the Snake man with her tenderness.

The Rabbit Woman with the Horse Man: This is a happy marriage. The Rabbit woman brings warmth and happiness to the family, which pleases the Horse man very much.

The Rabbit Woman with the Sheep Man: This is an average marriage. However, the Sheep man will focus more on the wealth of the Rabbit woman.

The Rabbit Woman with the Monkey Man: If the Rabbit woman is very careful in restraining the Monkey man, they will have a happy family.

The Rabbit Woman with the Rooster Man: The marriage will last forever if one of them is lenient towards the other. However, many of them tend to fail to do so.

The Rabbit Woman with the Dog Man: They can live together happily. The Rabbit woman can provide a tranquil and happy family for the Dog man.

The Rabbit Woman with the Pig Man: Everything will be happy and perfect. However, the Pig man is not supposed to have another woman outside the family and the Rabbit woman is supposed to be lenient towards such shortcomings of the Pig man.

The Luck of Wealth

People born in the Rabbit year enjoy a carefree life in old age with stable wealth. They should be more careful in the year of the Rooster, a year which is not good for making money and some "opportunities" are simply traps.

Herbal Medicine Pounded by the Jade Rabbit

As legend goes, three deities turned into three pitiful old men, begging for food from the Fox, the Monkey and the Rabbit. The Fox and the Monkey had food whereas the Rabbit had nothing. Later, the Rabbit said: "You can eat me!" Then it threw itself into the fire to be cooked. Greatly moved, three deities sent the Rabbit into the moon palace, turning it into the Jade Rabbit. The Jade Rabbit accompanied the Goddess of the Moon while pounding herbal medicine for longevity.

Overall Fortunes of the Rabbit
in Different Animal Years

The Year of the Rat: They are blessed with exceptional happiness and luck. There will be slight setbacks in the middle of the year, but a series of good lucks at the end of the year. While seeking for immense wealth and profits, they should be mindful of troubles caused by jealous people.

The Year of the Ox: As it is not smooth sailing in all things, they should be mindful of their health. Bad luck will recede slightly and some accomplishments will be made at the end of the year. They should seize opportunities to be happy so that bad luck will be off-set by good luck.

The Year of the Tiger: They need to be mindful of their health and everything else. It is not advisable to travel far away in the middle of the year. Bad luck will be gone at the end of the year, followed by good luck. Investment should be made when good luck comes around.

The Year of the Rabbit: Everything is smooth sailing, with prosperous business, fame, and wealth.

The Year of the Dragon: They should be exceptionally mindful in being conservative in their advance. Never make trouble! It is not advantageous to go seeking for wealth.

The Year of the Snake: They will be mentally disturbed and money-consuming to some extent. Such setbacks will recede after the middle of the year, gradually followed by prosperity and smooth sailing journey in career.

The Year of the Horse: There will be small setbacks at the beginning of the year, but a turn for the better after March. However, they will come across small problems. It is not advisable for them to be involved with other women and gambling.

The Year of the Sheep: They suffer from problems with operation and many obstacles in seeking wealth, resulting in small profits despite hard work throughout the year. Success can be made if they remain calm and sober-minded.

The Year of the Monkey: This is not a smooth sailing year,

The Complete Guide to Chinese Horoscopes

but problems still have solutions. It will be a peaceful year if they remain calm and sober-minded while engaging in undertakings.

The Year of the Rooster: They need to be more careful with enough mental preparation and firm will power, in addition to relying more on the help of relatives and friends.

The Year of the Dog: This is a year of very good destiny-oriented trends. They should be bent on engaging in undertakings and don't go too far in making money

The Year of the Pig: They should be particularly mindful about accidents. They need to be careful about safety, keep to themselves, and be cautious in contacting others.

Overall Fortunes of the Rabbit Born in Different Months by the Lunar Calendar

The 1st Lunar Month: Despite a comfortable life, they must travel around and work hard. This can be avoided if they are successful about what they do or plan their income and expenses well.

The 2nd Lunar Month: Despite ups and downs, they enjoy a comfortable life with fame and wealth.

The 3rd Lunar Month: They are bright, energetic, open-minded in their ways of thinking, and amazingly courageous. They have an ambitious future, brilliant career, and power.

The 4th Lunar Month: They are scholastic, elegant, knowledgeable, and versatile with a happy family. They enjoy happiness throughout life thanks to easy access to wealth and accomplish what they set out to achieve.

The 5th Lunar Month: Living in poverty in early years, they enjoy immense wealth in middle and old age. They are extremely good at building their career and very popular among their colleagues.

The 6th Lunar Month: With the amazing ability to lead with a dignified attitude, they are respected by people. They enjoy rapid career development, a happy family, and good health.

The 7th Lunar Month: They enjoy outstanding success in career and smooth sailing in everything. They are characterized by knowledge and intelligence as well as a noble and dignified personality, in addition to ample sources of wealth and a carefree life.

The 8th Lunar Month: With a kind heart and noble virtue, they are ready to help others and are greatly popular among people. They would be well-known if they serve as local officials in their community.

The 9th Lunar Month: Without an enterprising spirit, they are indifferent to all things, submitting themselves to the will of God. Despite a carefree life, they are not very wealthy.

The 10th Lunar Month: Introverted and not very social, they still encounter some dangerous things. However, danger is ward off since they will have the help of others.

The 11th Lunar Month: Versatile and ingenious, they pay more attention to brotherhood than wealth. In their early years, they are able to make money, with all things to their satisfaction. In old age, they enjoy both wealth and longevity.

The 12th Lunar Month: Resourceful and highly ambitious, they work hard at study in childhood, followed by fame, gains, and immense wealth. After middle age, they will have to work hard to enjoy prosperity.

Overall Fortunes of the Rabbit Born on Different Days by the Lunar Calendar

The 1st Day: Bright, active, loyal, and dignified, they pay more attention to brotherhood than wealth, always ready to help others.

The 2nd Day: Despite many ups and downs as well as troubles in their early years, they are loyal and honest.

The 3rd Day: They suffer from tragedies in their early years and seldom have good luck in their youth. They will have to start from the bottom and work their way up in their career.

The 4th Day: They are hard-working, with satisfaction in their family and accomplishments in their career. They often change their residence. They will advance in their career without family support.

The 5th Day: Experiencing both bitterness and sweetness, they find it easy in their career development after going through difficulties. They are resilient and benevolent.

The 6th Day: Innately loyal and honest, they are kind-hearted, popular among people, dignified in their actions and thoughtful in taking care of their family.

The 7th Day: Bright, smart, devoted, and consistent, they are talented with a comfortable life. They are fond of making friends.

The 8th Day: With sweetness coming after bitterness, they experience hardship in gaining wealth in their early years and their good luck comes after middle age.

The 9th Day: Loyal and honest throughout their life, they do things in a down-to-earth manner. With an ordinary life in their early years, they go through hardship before embarking on a smooth sailing journey.

The 10th Day: They have a carefree life and are lucky in marriage, family, and career.

The 11th Day: Experiencing hardship in their early years, they will not have help from relatives and friends. It is better for them to seek wealth far away from home.

The 12th Day: With both fame and wealth, they enjoy success and development.

The 13th Day: Despite their outstanding wisdom and immense resourcefulness, they are hot-tempered and not as enterprising.

The 14th Day: Bright and highly adaptable, they often come across difficulties.

The 15th Day: With both bitterness and sweetness, they experience bad luck in their early years.

The 16th Day: The husband and wife respect each other.

The 17th Day: Bright and beautiful, they are helped by many people. With ordinary luck in their early years, they enjoy prosperity in middle age.

The 18th Day: With sound moral integrity and respect from others, they come across good luck in middle age.

The 19th Day: With sweetness coming after bitterness and a smooth sailing journey coming after difficulties, they will have to paddle their own canoes to become prosperous after middle age.

The 20th Day: Ambitious and strong-willed, they do things resolutely.

The 21st Day: With an unsupportive family background, it is better for them to try to be successful away from home.

The 22nd Day: Hard-working and resilient, they have a happy family thanks to their diligence, thrift, and kindness.

The 23rd Day: Bright, ingenious, and good-tempered, they are popular among people.

The 24th Day: With a rather calm road after enduring some difficulties, they work hard in their early years and develop their career away from home.

The 25th Day: They live a carefree life with quite favorable conditions in their early years. However, they have an average life in middle age, with the usual problems and worries.

The 26th Day: Bright and outstandingly skillful, they are blessed with glory throughout life. They live stably in the old age and enjoy longevity.

The 27th Day: Bright and eager to learn, they are characterized by extraordinary intelligence. They are blessed with glory throughout life, making their family proud. They enjoy a happy marriage, along with lots of wealth and gains.

The 28th Day: Marriage is a happy one and they will come across helpful people when they are away from home. They are flexible in handling relations with others and always enjoy success, fame, prosperity, and longevity.

The 29th Day: Great luck! The man is handsome with a successful career. The woman is bright and kind and adept at running the household.

The 30th Day: By working hard, they become successful after middle age with a great career and family, as well as immense wealth. They will enjoy comfort and longevity in old age.

Overall Fortunes of the Rabbit Born in Different Hours

11 PM–1 AM: They are mostly happy and romantic, paying no attention to family or marriage. Most of them are fond of the new and tired of the old. There will be no happy marriage unless they are mindful of controlling their flightiness.

1 AM–3 AM: Smart, ingenious, open-minded, and highly ambitious, they are successful in their studies in childhood. Resourceful, diligent, and thrifty, they can rely on their family members and relatives while being good at making friends. They marry, have their own business, and enjoy glory in middle age. They live peacefully in old age.

3 AM–5 AM: Upright and capable, they start from the bottom up in their career. They work hard in their early years, become successful away from home, and enjoy a stability in the old age.

Two Chinese Parasol Trees and Two Rabbits

Height: 176.2 cm. Width: 95 cm.
Ink and color on silk
Beijing Palace Museum

This is a painting by Leng Mei (1670–1742), a painter of the Qing court. There are two Chinese parasol trees with an osmanthus tree protruding slantingly from the rock-chink. In addition, there are chrysanthemum flowers all over the ground, with two rabbits playing amidst soft grass. It is seemingly a painting for the mid-autumn festival.

Two rabbits are accurately shaped with vivid images, as well as shining and sleek fur of true-to-life texture. Their eyes look crystal clear and transparent as they are dotted in white with reflection. Rocks appear hard and steep. The entire picture is reasonably laid out, with meticulous brushwork, attention to the texture as well as harmonious and gorgeous contrast of colors, obviously under the influence of Western painting techniques.

5 AM–7 AM: Resourceful, fierce, knowledgeable, and versatile in defiance of power and hardship, they are extraordinarily courageous, hence becoming famous and making their family proud.

7 AM–9 AM: Bright, capable, talented, and knowledgeable, they work hard for fame throughout life. In the end, they have more failures than successes. Their biggest weakness is characterized by the lack of a well-designed and detailed action plan, hence leading to working hard in vain. It is not until middle age that they begin to see the lessons in their failures.

9 AM–11 AM: They work hard throughout life, with no family members and relatives to rely on. They are free from serious problems and work hard to build a career.

11 AM–1 PM: With the help of others, their bad luck can be turned into opportunities. They are both attractive in appearance and talented. The man can marry a beautiful wife while the woman can marry a talented husband. They love each other and live happily throughout their life.

1 PM–3 PM: Exceptionally bright, they are well educated. With the help from their family, they will enjoy a brilliant career. They should be mindful of other people they come in contact with.

3 PM–5 PM: With lots of ups and downs, they can have bad luck turn into opportunities, without serious tragedies or problems.

5 PM–7 PM: They are versatile, capable, and ingenious. They will not be able to get married or establish a career unless they stay away from home and they will be helped by people in other places. They are not able to make money in their early years, but will see some improvement after forty years old.

7 PM–9 PM: Despite ups and downs as well as many tragedies and problems in their life, they can overcome them safe and sound.

9 PM–11 PM: They experience many ups and downs. However, because of having a good family foundation with helpful parents and brothers, they can avoid unnecessary setbacks as long as they adjust their principles of action at all times.

Chapter Five
The Dragon

In Chinese culture, the Dragon enjoys the most supreme status. It is respected and worshiped. It stands for power, nobility, greatness, good luck, optimism, and success. In feudal dynasties, the Dragon was the exclusive use of royalty. It could never be used by the public. The emperor was known as the "ordained son of the true Dragon" and his descendants were the "off-springs of the Dragon." In the Chinese zodiac, the Dragon ranks fifth and represents nobility.

Lunar Years of the Dragon in the Solar Calendar

5 February 1916 to 3 February 1917

5 February 1928 to 3 February 1929

5 February 1940 to 3 February 1941

5 February 1952 to 3 February 1953

5 February 1964 to 3 February 1965

4 February 1976 to 3 February 1977

4 February 1988 to 3 February 1989

4 February 2000 to 3 February 2001

4 February 2012 to 2 February 2013

4 February 2024 to 2 February 2025

4 February 2036 to 2 February 2037

4 February 2048 to 2 February 2049

Life Path

People born in the Dragon year are robust, energetic, exceedingly bold, and have an incredible temper. They possess broad ambitions and the ability to lead with a strong self-confidence and an indomitable spirit. They are innately lucky people with favorable access to success in their career. Whatever they do, they don't like being ordered about and enjoy paddling their own canoes. In their teens, they need to avoid being trapped in stubbornness and failure. In their middle age, they need to avoid troubles caused by illegal undertakings. They will enjoy happiness in their old age.

Personality

Dragon people are frank, strong-willed, and exceptionally enterprising with a balance of street smarts and intelligence. Those born in the daytime are highly focused with an abundance of spirit to fight or defend and the ability to take the bull by the horns. Those born at night are marked by perfection, but lack persistence and will power. They are not capable of withstanding tests. They need to have an indomitable spirit in order to get success in their career and love.

Profession

Due to their strong enterprising spirit and innate intelligence, it is not suitable for them to engage in jobs that do not require thought, such as manual labor and mechanical operation. They tend to choose jobs where they can demonstrate their creativity and analytical skills. They are fond of taking part in spiritual activities concerned with art, politics, and academia.

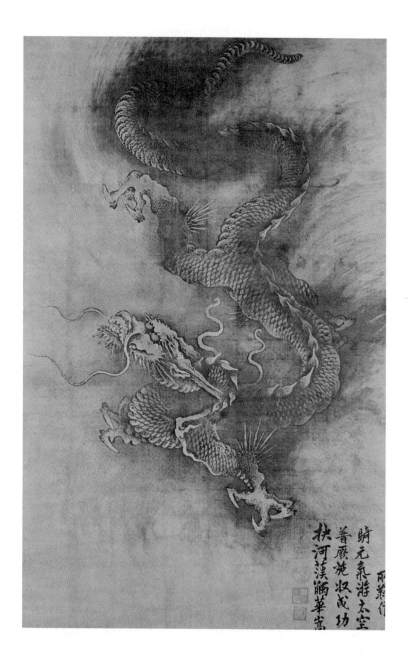

Love and Marriage

Most of them are faithful to their families. They put much important emphasis on the concept of marriage. They succeed easily if they're in a supportive marriage. However, they should bear in mind not to be too stubborn and should listen often to the suggestions of their spouse. They are suitably matched with people born in the year of the Rat, the Rooster, and the Monkey. They should be careful with those of the Rabbit, the Dog, the Ox and the Dragon.

Marriage Compatibility with Women Born in Other Animal Years

The Dragon Man with the Rat Woman: This is a happy match. The wife is supportive and will be of great help to her husband's career.

The Dragon Man with the Ox Woman: This is not a very happy match, because the husband yearns for a tenderness that his

The Dragon amidst Clouds

Preserved in the Museum of Guangdong Province in China, it was painted by Chen Rong in the Southern Song Dynasty (1127–1279). On the base joined by two pieces of thin silk, there is a huge dragon amidst clouds whirling upward majestically. As the legend goes, the Dragon is one of the four spirits and the deity in charge of the rain. It is featured by the deer antler, the fish scales, the rabbit eyes, the ox-ears, the tiger-palms, and the eagle claws. In the Han Dynasty and the Tang Dynasty (618–907), it was mostly in the form of beasts, but gradually in the form of snakes after the Song Dynasty. This painting can be regarded a typical dragon painting. In addition to having laid foundation for the form of Dragon in the following several hundred years, it is also almost incomparable in expressing the Dragon in the following generation.

wife will not be able to provide.

The Dragon Man with the Tiger Woman: This is a fairly happy match.

The Dragon Man with the Rabbit Woman: There will be some conflicts, because the wife is fond of showing off and the husband is suspicious of every superficial thing.

The Dragon Man with the Dragon Woman: There will be many arguments and troubles.

The Dragon Man with the Snake Woman: This is a very suitable match. The husband is proud of his beautiful wife. However, the wife's attempts to be beautiful is not necessarily for the benefit of her husband.

The Dragon Man with the Horse Woman: Everything will go smoothly in the pursuit of their desires and goals, but sustaining them will be an issue.

The Dragon Man with the Sheep Woman: They are quite happy together despite the marriage not being beneficial to the career development of the husband.

The Dragon Man with the Monkey Woman: This is absolutely a perfect marriage. The wife offers useful advice to her husband about his career, helping him to correct his over confidence.

The Dragon Man with the Rooster Woman: They will live together happily and have an enviable family life.

The Dragon Man with the Dog Woman: Their family life will not be peaceful, because the wife is often irritated by her husband's conceitedness.

The Dragon Man with the Pig Woman: They will live together happily. The wife is very empathetic to her husband.

Marriage Compatibility with Men Born in Other Animal Years

The Dragon Woman with the Rat Man: They will live together quite happily. The wife is able to satisfy her husband's vanity.

The Dragon Woman with the Ox Man: There will be some conflicts, because the wife is fond of showing off and the husband is suspicious of every superficial thing.

The Dragon Woman with the Tiger Man: This is a fairly happy match. The wife will be a great help to her husband's career.

The Dragon Woman with the Rabbit Man: They are sweet to one another, but the wife should take responsibility of the housework.

The Dragon Woman with the Dragon Man: There will be many arguments and troubles.

The Dragon Woman with the Snake Man: It is quite difficult for them to have a peaceful life since they can easily get into confrontations.

The Dragon Woman with the Horse Man: This is not an ideal marriage. The husband is self-centered, often disregarding his wife's feelings.

The Dragon Woman with the Sheep Man: This marriage can only work if both make efforts to appreciate each other.

The Dragon Woman with the Monkey Man: They can live together peacefully. The wife will always be appreciative of her husband's appearance.

The Dragon Woman with the Rooster Man: This is a perfect marriage.

The Dragon Woman with the Dog Man: This is not a suitable marriage. The husband will always find faults with his wife.

The Dragon Woman with the Pig Man: They can live together peacefully, but the husband will have to sacrifice his career.

The Luck of Wealth

People born in the Dragon year are extremely intelligent and have a talent for leadership. However, most of them are hot-tempered and often encounter competitors, easily resulting in disadvantages against the development of their career and pursuit of wealth. They will enjoy better developments if they pay more attention to cultivating themselves spiritually. In regards to the pursuit of wealth, the years of the Rooster and Rooster people are the most advantageous to the Dragon.

Overall Fortunes of the Dragon in Different Animal Years

The Year of the Rat: They are in the prime of wealth and gains without any obstacles. After July, they should prevent accidents from taking place and never engage in gambling.

The Year of the Ox: All things are optimistic. They can make a business investment at the appropriate time. However, they should try to gain more information and act with caution.

The Year of the Tiger: They work hard far away from home. Though they enjoy an abundance of wealth, they are tired from their hard work.

The Year of the Rabbit: They enjoy small gains at the end of the year as reward for their hard work. They should behave themselves and never engage in gambling.

The Year of the Dragon: They have opportunities for further study and will be successful. There will be obstacles in the middle of the year that will require more caution.

The Year of the Snake: More caution is required and attention should be paid to nourishing the body and exercising.

The Year of the Horse: Nothing is smooth sailing and there are small setbacks. There will be slight improvement at the end of the year, but caution is still needed.

The Year of the Sheep: Problems should be handled calmly and right and wrong should be distinguished clearly so as to ensure peace.

The Year of the Monkey: It is better to make plans in the beginning of the year. It is advisable to stay low-key in the middle of the year and pursue wealth at the end of the year. There will be unexpected wealth, but don't be greedy.

The Year of the Rooster: All things are smooth sailing with a lot of optimism. However, there will be minor illness and a small loss of wealth. Everything will be fine as long as they stay calm and peaceful.

The Year of the Dog: Misunderstanding or troubles resulting from gossips are unavoidable and there will be failed plans. Don't be rapacious and greedy, a peaceful life is attainable.

The Year of the Pig: All things are smooth sailing and every success can be made. However, caution is required at the beginning of the year.

The Nine-Dragon Wall

As one of the screen walls, it serves to block the view in traditional Chinese buildings. The Nine-Dragon Wall in Beihai Park in Beijing is the most characteristic one. Built in 1756, it is 5 meters high, 1.2 meters thick and 27 meters long. Among the nine dragons, the middle one is called the prime dragon in its typical resting position, flanked by the rising dragons and falling dragons respectively. Nine dragons fly majestically in different postures. The prime dragon appears majestic and dignified, the rising dragons look fierce and forceful, and the falling dragons seem mild and elegant. They stand for harmonious cooperation, perfection and flourishing world.

Jade Dragon

Length: 26 cm. Overall width: 21 cm. Diameter of section: 2.3–2.9 cm.
Diameter of hole: 0.95 cm. Color: black / green.
Ornamental jade of the Hongshan culture
Sanxingtala, Ogniud Banner, Inner Mongolia Autonomous Region
National Museum of China

The earliest jades in the shape of dragons appeared in the
Hongshan culture of 6,500–5,000 years ago. This dragon jade is in
the form of a reversed letter C, the upper lip protrudes slightly and
the mouth is tightly closed but thrust forward. The nose is flat with a
sharp ridge along its length .There are two small nostrils and ridged
eyes. The eyebrows stand out like the teeth of a comb. The forehead
and the jaw are both finely carved with a rhomboid lattice pattern.

There is a long mane on the back of the neck which flows
in a curve towards the rear, the two edges form a blunt blade and
there is a concave groove on either side .The dragon's narrow body
is curved inwards and the tail is curled. There is a small hole on
the back of the dragon as if for threading a cord for suspending the
jade so that the head and tail are at the same level.

This piece is carved in the round shape from a complete piece
of jade and is the earliest known jade dragon known as "China's first
dragon." Some people believe that it was a clan emblem or totem.

Overall Fortunes of the Dragon Born in Different Months by the Lunar Calendar

The 1st Lunar Month: Despite their ambition and high ideals, as well as the ability to become a VIP, there is no opportunity to display them. They have to rely on themselves, making it difficult to accomplish career goals.

The 2nd Lunar Month: Smart and intelligent and well-educated, they are free from serious troubles. They enjoy a thriving career, endless source of wealth and prosperity and are respected by lots of people. They have many children.

The 3rd Lunar Month: Attractive, smart, knowledgeable, ambitious, courageous, resourceful, and strong-willed, they have a talent for organization and leadership. They will enjoy respect, success, and fame.

The 4th Lunar Month: Robust, energetic, righteous, unrestrained, and frank, they have a deep hatred for unethical practice. They have phenomenal aspirations and extraordinary talents.

The 5th Lunar Month: They have an innate talent to get along well with others. They will quickly become officials and make notable accomplishments. Their wealth luck is extraordinary. However, they are hot-tempered and eccentric.

The 6th Lunar Month: Despite lots of knowledge and intelligence, they don't have much help from others and accomplishing things will be difficult because timing is very awkward. Their business is mixed with advantages and disadvantages and their life goes through ups and downs from time to time.

The 7th Lunar Month: With courage, insight, and great intelligence, they enjoy a prosperous career. However, they need to pay attention to their temper and their leadership style to prevent setbacks.

The 8th Lunar Month: Knowledgeable and talented, they are content with the present status quo, unwilling to work hard. They are lazy, which is an undesirable habit. They are fond of living alone. However, they are free from serious problems throughout life.

The 9th Lunar Month: Mild, faithful, honest, and composed, they are helped by others and are successful without serious troubles. They are strong-willed and courageous after failure, always optimistic with every new start. Therefore, they enjoy happiness and comfort throughout life.

The 10th Lunar Month: Smart, attractive, elegant, and outstandingly talented, they are admired and respected by others. With courage and insight, they are helped by many people, so they are able to turn a bad situation into a beneficial one and make success. They enjoy happiness throughout life thanks to an endless influx of wealth.

The 11th Lunar Month: Despite having exceptional talents and ambitions, they seldom have opportunities. They either miss them or fall prey to the tricks of people with ulterior motives. They should make more friends and work out thoughtful plans to gradually implement in order to become successful.

The 12th Lunar Month: They have no relatives to rely on and lack help from others, so they tend to work harder with less gain. It they don't mind struggling and learn to make friends who are capable, then there is hope for success.

Overall Fortunes of the Dragon Born on Different Days by the Lunar Calendar

The 1st Day: They are helped by others, blessed with a smooth life and great opportunities.

The 2nd Day: Starting from scratch, they seek wealth away from home and will find success and prosperity.

The 3rd Day: With sound morality and a positive outlook, they have accomplishments in early years, followed by the establishment of a family and a successful career with notable fame.

The 4th Day: Plagued with poor health, they find it difficult to use their talents. They could suffer from depression throughout life.

The 5th Day: Smart, enthusiastic about learning, and articulate, they have the potential to be successful if they take care to mind troubles.

The 6th Day: Full of troubles, they find success difficult and experience significant ups and downs.

The 7th Day: They are often helped by strangers and relatives. They will have a happy marriage and life is filled with more joy than worries.

The 8th Day: They are smart and enthusiastic about learning, and they will have more success than failures. Capable of managing the family well, the Dragon woman is a great helper to the husband.

The 9th Day: Capable of convincing others, they are able to become success with immense wealth.

The 10th Day: Though not wealthy, they will have an adventurous life. They will get a continuous influx of small gains.

The 11th Day: With an unstable income, they spend as much as they earn. Throughout life, they are fond of making friends and spend money like water.

The 12th Day: Both the Dragon man and woman will have supportive and desirable spouses. Thanks to the help from their spouses, they will always have money and wealth, in addition to having many children.

The 13th Day: They are known for accomplishing their tasks with extraordinary results, so they will have a successful career. They will also have devoted sons and daughters.

The 14th Day: They are in a position to inherit the legacy and help from their family. Their early life will be quiet, but they will enjoy immense luck after middle age.

The 15th Day: Most of them will work hard away from home. The Dragon woman enjoys a promising marriage with both sons and daughters as well as a comfortable life.

The 16th Day: Innately smart, diligent, and enthusiastic about learning, they enjoy a prosperous family and career with ample wealth.

The 17th Day: Blessed with a promising marriage, they are helped by others when it comes to making money, which results in a stable and peaceful life.

The 18th Day: With help from parents, they don't have to work so hard. They enjoy a comfortable life though they find it difficult to make a lot of money.

The 19th Day: They suffer from troubles and loss of wealth, resulting in more failures than successes. They are not on good terms with relatives, so they do not have help from them.

The 20th Day: Kind-hearted with a firm temperament, they are fond of showing off. They enjoy a stable and successful career development.

The 21st Day: Kind-hearted, both the Dragon man and the Dragon woman are devoted to their parents. They will both have supportive spouses.

The 22nd Day: The Dragon man is likely to attract a lot of women due to his fondness for dating. With a romantic personality, the Dragon woman enjoys singing and dancing, thus living a happy life.

The 23rd Day: They find it impossible to rely on relatives, so they must start from scratch to seek career development away from home.

The 24th Day: Success and a promising career with a bright future is expected.

The 25th Day: Intelligent and smart with exceptional skills, they will enjoy success and fame.

The 26th Day: Narrow-minded and particular about everything, they fail to make any significant achievements in their career. The Dragon woman enjoys a much more comfortable life with better luck than the Dragon man.

The 27th Day: Working long and hard all day long, they barely eke out a living and experience significant ups and downs.

The 28th Day: They will have a prosperous family and career, along with a peaceful marriage and a comfortable life.

The 29th Day: They find it difficult to make their dreams come true. Some are poor and some are rich. Caution is needed to prevent troubles with the opposite sex.

The 30th Day: With extraordinary talents, they will be notable leaders and live a wonderful life.

Emperor Kangxi in the Dragon Robe

The dragon robe is named after the dragon pattern on the robe which was worn by the emperor in attending ceremonies in ancient times. It is marked by the round collars, left front overlapping right front, and the yellow color. Kangxi (May 4, 1654–December 20, 1722) was the fourth emperor of the Qing Dynasty. He ascended the throne at eight and began to handle state affairs at 14. Being the emperor for 61 years, he was the emperor of the longest royal service in the history of China. Kangxi defended unified China from multi-ethnic groups and laid the foundation for the prosperity of the Qing Dynasty, having created a grand situation of thriving times under himself and Emperor Qianlong.

Overall Fortunes of the Dragon Born in Different Hours

11 PM–1 AM: With all things being promising, they will enjoy a magnificently successful career.

1 AM–3 AM: With great luck, they will take on magnificent projects and business ventures that will yield outstanding results.

3 AM–5 AM: Working all over the country, they seldom stay at home. Caution is always required in doing things.

5 AM–7 AM: Success cannot be made unless great efforts are exerted.

7 AM–9 AM: Respected by others, they enjoy a comfortable life and always attain success whenever they strive for it.

9 AM–11 AM: Whatever they do, their path will always be smooth.

11 AM–1 PM: As they are bound to come across some difficulties, they need to be cautious in doing things in order to bring good luck to their family.

1 PM–3 PM: Working all over the country, they come across lots of troubles and problems, but also enjoy opportunities for success.

3 PM–5 PM: Despite a wealthy life, they often come across problems in their career that requires caution.

5 PM–7 PM: They are apt to attract people of the opposite sex, which requires caution. Attention should be paid to preventing misunderstanding or troubles caused by gossip. Despite wealth and gains, they also suffer from troubles and worries.

7 PM–9 PM: Attention should be paid to prevent misunderstanding or troubles caused by gossip. Sometimes, they will suffer from a small loss of wealth, so caution is required.

9 PM–11 PM: Being virtuous, they enjoy very good luck and can always turn bad situations around. They seldom have to worry because most things end up working out to their benefit.

Chapter Six
The Snake

People have contradictory feelings about the Snake. They fear and worship it at the same time, making it one of the most controversial animals in the Chinese zodiac. The Snake ranks sixth and represents mystery and wisdom.

Lunar Years of the Snake in the Solar Calendar

4 February 1917 to 3 February 1918

4 February 1929 to 3 February 1930

4 February 1941 to 3 February 1942

4 February 1953 to 3 February 1954

4 February 1965 to 3 February 1966

4 February 1977 to 3 February 1978

4 February 1989 to 3 February 1990

4 February 2001 to 3 February 2002

3 February 2013 to 3 February 2014

3 February 2025 to 3 February 2026

3 February 2037 to 3 February 2038

Life Path

People born in the year of the Snake have a mysterious, romantic, and seemingly gentle appearance. They conduct themselves with sophistication and possess a calmness, but underneath all that composure is a fighting spirit. Instead of showing off, they covertly go about their business to gradually advance their plans. Innately perceptive and knowledgeable, they tend to get the upper hand at work with the goal to create a successful career for themselves. However, they lack the spirit of cooperation, so they often experience failure. As intellectuals, they always think twice before doing things. They know their own abilities very well. Their spiritual life is very important. They have a sixth sense and superb insight. They will suffer from many failures in their early years, but old age will be a happy one.

Personality

The Snake is good at observation, a great problem solver, and is highly adaptable. Despite a plain personality, they can make decision resolutely. Their shortcomings are marked by an anti-social personality with considerable cunning.

Profession

The Snake enjoys a successful career and many business opportunities. They need to have a systematic plan for gradual involvement and perfection. Their acute feelings and unique personality usually enable them to have their own ways of working so they seldom consider the ideas of others. They are fond of jobs associated with intellectual thinking and are against jobs that are too mechanical or monotonous.

Nüwa Patches up the Sky

According to a legend in Chinese mythology, a female deity with a human head and a snake-like body is called Nüwa. As it is said, after the propagation of human beings, the water deity fought against the fire deity all of a sudden and gave rise to the fall of half of the sky and a huge hole, causing unprecedented disaster to mankind. Nüwa was determined to end this disaster by patching up the sky. She chose stones of five colors, burnt them into thick liquid to be filled into the huge hole. Then, she chopped off four feet of a big turtle to be used as four pillars to support the fallen half of the sky. As a result, people began to return to peaceful life.

Love and Marriage

When coming into contact with the Snake for the first time, some are afraid of their indifferent personality. However, as time goes on, people find that the Snake is actually very sentimental and passionate. They are strict and discriminating. It is not easy for them to accept the ideas of others. However, they enjoy a smooth, happy family life, as well as a love life. They are suitably matched with people born in the year of the Ox, the Rooster and the Monkey. They should be careful with those of the Tiger and the Pig.

Marriage Compatibility with Women Born in Other Animal Years

The Snake Man with the Rat Woman: An ideal marriage is almost impossible since there is a lack of rational thinking.

The Snake Man with the Ox Woman: This is a happy marriage. The husband is willing to go along with the ideas of his wife.

The Snake Man with the Tiger Woman: This is not a happy marriage, since there are many differences between them in regards to opinions and interests.

The Snake Man with the Rabbit Woman: This is a calm and

balanced marriage. Both are very realistic, yet they have a bit of the romantic in them.

The Snake Man with the Dragon Woman: For the marriage to lasts, it is better not to be around one another every day.

The Snake Man with the Snake Woman: They can live together peacefully if they respect and love each other.

The Snake Man with the Horse Woman: It is very difficult for them to rely on each other.

The Snake Man with the Sheep Woman: This is a perfect marriage.

The Snake Man with the Monkey Woman: They can co-exist peacefully.

The Snake Man with the Rooster Woman: This is innately a perfect marriage. The honesty and openness of the wife brings about harmony between them.

The Snake Man with the Dog Woman: Their relationship fails to grow despite their efforts, because they have completely different beliefs in life.

The Snake Man with the Pig Woman: Though this is not a very nice marriage, the kind-heartedness of the wife can change her husband's flirtatious nature.

Marriage Compatibility with Men Born in Other Animal Years

The Snake Woman with the Rat Man: They can co-exist peacefully only by taking responsibility for each other.

The Snake Woman with the Ox Man: They can co-exist peacefully as long as the wife can make some concessions to her husband.

The Snake Woman with the Tiger Man: Conflicts take place easily if both sides cannot reach mutual understanding of each other.

The Snake Woman with the Rabbit Man: They can co-exist peacefully if they are both mature in their ways of thinking.

The Snake Woman with the Dragon Man: This is a perfect marriage.

The Snake Woman with the Snake Man: They can co-exist peacefully if they respect and love each other.

The Snake Woman with the Horse Man: This is a happy marriage. The wife brings a lot of warmth and happiness to her family.

The Snake Woman with the Sheep Man: Unremitting efforts on both sides can keep their family life balanced.

The Snake Woman with the Monkey Man: They can co-exist peacefully.

The Snake Woman with the Rooster Man: Both are well-educated and polite. They complement each other, leading to a fairly nice marriage.

The Snake Woman with the Dog Man: They can happily co-exist.

The Snake Woman with the Pig Man: They need to find the good in each other and value their relationship.

The Luck of Wealth

With fairly good luck of wealth, people of the Snake never worry about money which is made not necessarily through their work, but unexpectedly. Most of the money comes from some speculative gains. Since their childhood, they have formed luxurious ways of life, i.e. they never buy inexpensive things. They should practice economy and spend money on profitable speculative undertakings.

Overall Fortunes of the Snake in Different Animal Years

The Year of the Rat: With optimistic opportunities, they will get to accomplish a lot in their career. However, they should not get carried away by success.

The Year of the Ox: Due to many factors that are out of their control, they should be cautious and do more good deeds in order to ensure peace.

The Year of the Tiger: They will come across many adversities and obstacles in business and other things. Therefore, they should be open-minded and lenient toward others.

The Year of the Rabbit: They are helped by other people despite their bad luck. Their luck will turn around at the end of the year with promising opportunities on the way.

The Year of the Dragon: They will make money and score career achievements.

The Year of the Snake: They must be cautious while making friends. They should be conservative to some extent in their career development at the end of the year. For peace, advance or retreat whatever the case may be.

The Year of the Horse: This is a gloomy year. Troubles can be resolved as long as they are kind and generous. At the end of the year, they will have free rein to take their initiative over their gains. Caution is required in doing everything and greed should be tempered.

The Year of the Sheep: There will be obstacles at the beginning of the year, but things will turn for the better in the mid-year. Stability will develop at the end of the year. They should spend more time with family members. Only good developments will take place at the right time, in the right place, and with the right people.

The Year of the Monkey: Keep calm and be adaptable under any circumstance.

The Year of the Rooster: They will enjoy a smooth career and a good amount of wealth. Despite encounters with people with ulterior motives at the end of the year, they will still persevere.

The Year of the Dog: Whenever there is an opportunity to go away from home, they should seize this opportunity to develop their career. They are likely to make a lot of good friends, employ honest and reliable people, and win over them with fringe benefits.

The Year of the Pig: They should not go too far despite good wealth luck. They should remain kind and not be greedy in spite of their wealth.

Legend of the White Snake

As the legend goes, Bai Suzhen was a snake spirit cultivated through one thousand years. In order to repay a debt of gratitude to a young scholar Xu Xian for saving her life, she turned into a human being. She managed ingeniously to get acquainted with Xu Xian and marry him. However, after their marriage, the monk Fahai taught Xu Xian to disclose the original form of his wife. For this, Bai Suzhen struggled against the monk who brought her into a magic earthen bowl and subdued her under Leifeng Pagoda (Hangzhou City, Zhejiang Province). Later, Bai Suzhen's son became number one in the Imperial Examination. Coming to the pagoda to offer sacrifices, he rescued his mother, finally resulting in the family reunion.

This painting is shown on the wall of a long veranda in Summer Palace, the royal garden of the Qing Dynasty. It is the longest veranda of ancient buildings and gardens in China. Each square beam is decorated with a colorful painting. There are totally over 14,000 paintings of bright color and great magnificence. Painting on buildings has long been a traditional craftsmanship in China. Wood is mostly used as construction materials for ancient Chinese buildings. The paint of these paintings actually plays a role of protecting the materials.

Overall Fortunes of the Snake Born in Different Months by the Lunar Calendar

The 1st Lunar Month: Despite hard work and great ambition, it is difficult to reach their objectives due to their lack of talents. Worse still, they don't have help from others, making it impossible for them to achieve great success. They should work normal jobs and give up the dream of becoming rich overnight. Otherwise, they will lose more than what they gain.

The 2nd Lunar Month: Though highly educated, they are not very wealthy. They can become successful in their career if they go about things in an orderly way. However, they are not able to accomplish much since they do not have great ideals and ambitions.

The 3rd Lunar Month: Smart, intelligent, knowledgeable, and versatile with ideals and ambitions, they are flexible and wise in doing things. Despite being from a poor family, they are able to start from the bottom and work their way up to become the foundation of their organization and community.

The 4th Lunar Month: With immense prosperity and help from others, they possess outstanding resourcefulness and talents. As officials, they hold power. As craftsmen, they are famous. With a lofty sense of justice, they have great ideals and ambitions, being able to accomplish whatever they set their sights on.

The 5th Lunar Month: Smart, intelligent, knowledgeable, and versatile, they are also strong-willed with outstanding courage and insight. They are philosophical and sees the bigger picture, being very good at taking the situation into consideration and seizing opportunities. With help from others, they enjoy peace, influence, and power.

The 6th Lunar Month: With immense prosperity, they are known for their virtues, power, and wealth. They have a lot of respect from other people and support from family members. They are honest and sincere toward others, strong-willed, and daring when it comes to overcoming difficulties. Moreover, they are very nice cooperators with very strong leadership capability.

The 7th Lunar Month: With outstanding intelligence, talents, wisdom, and courage, they can overcome adversity. They are very good at doing business, with an endless influx of wealth.

The 8th Lunar Month: They are faithful, reliable, kind-hearted, easy-going, morally sound, respectful, and devoted to their parents. They get along well with others and are respected by people. They are free from serious troubles throughout life.

The 9th Lunar Month: They are helped by others when working away from home, which enables them to develop a family and career. Throughout life, they are free from serious troubles and feel content at the age of 40.

The 10th Lunar Month: Kind-hearted and honest, they are fond of helping others. They will not have any serious troubles throughout life.

The 11th Lunar Month: Out-spoken and talented, they don't bully others and fear nothing. They make their own plans and work away from home to develop their career. They come across adversities in their youth, but good luck comes in middle age, and a peaceful life is expected in old age.

The 12th Lunar Month: With a neutral personality, they are consistent in doing things. In their early years, they are unlucky due to a poor family background. They will enjoy stability after 40 years old and a contentment after 50 years old.

Overall Fortunes of the Snake Born on Different Days by the Lunar Calendar

The 1st Day: Their destiny is good luck. They will experience a smooth life filled with many happy events and their successes will outnumber their failures.

The 2nd Day: Smart and versatile, they lead an ordinary life in their early years, but enjoy prosperity in old age.

The 3rd Day: They will enjoy happiness in their old age after experiencing many ups and downs in their early life. They should not expect help from brothers or other relatives.

The 4th Day: They are careless in making friends, so suffer at hands of their friends easily. They should be mindful of their moods, because they will be frustrated and lose their wealth.

The 5th Day: They are light-hearted and will come across many happy events and enjoy themselves. They should be mindful of external influence, which can cause divorce and hurt feelings, not to mention a loss of wealth.

The 6th Day: They are blessed with opportunities and cursed with bad luck. However, they will become wealthy, have a family, and develop a successful career if they stay away from home.

The 7th Day: They will suffer from many emotional problems. They should be mindful of the complete loss of money and lack of care in old age.

The 8th Day: With both happiness and worries, they will experience misfortunes in their early years and frequent problems. They will work hard in their youth and suffer from many ups and downs.

The 9th Day: They are prone to get into trouble, encounter more adversities than favors in doing things. Therefore, they should be mindful of a big loss of wealth.

The 10th Day: They will be powerful and influential, with lots of sources of business and ample wealth.

The 11th Day: Their tirelessly hard work will yield a balanced amount of happiness and worries throughout life.

The 12th Day: They are destined to work from the bottom up, but it will be better if they move away from home as they will be more than likely to succeed on their own.

The 13th Day: Romantic and joyful, they lead an ordinary life in their early years, but are blessed with good luck in middle age. However, there will be many problems in old age.

The 14th Day: With a happy marriage and a supportive spouse, they are expected to enjoy a successful career and the development of a very comfortable life.

The 15th Day: With a smooth career, they will find it easy to make a fortune and have a big family. However, they should be mindful of problems.

The 16th Day: Without relatives and friends, they should be mindful of troubles.

The 17th Day: With outstanding fame, they make their family proud.

The 18th Day: They enjoy a prosperous family and ample wealth. Their off-springs are devoted.

The 19th Day: Despite hard work, they enjoy happiness, a comfortable life, and considerable fame.

The 20th Day: They enjoy a prosperous family, ample wealth, immense fame, and gains.

The 21st Day: With unfortunate luck in their early years, the tide will turn in middle age, with prosperity as their destiny.

The 22nd Day: Working as officials away from home, they enjoy good luck in middle age and live a comfortable life.

The 23rd Day: Smart and knowledgeable with extraordinary courage and insight, they will have an easy life with many career achievements.

The 24th Day: Attracting people of the opposite sex, they enjoy lots of happiness in their life, but without accumulating much wealth.

The 25th Day: Smart, intelligent, and talented, they enjoy outstanding fame and prosperity.

The 26th Day: Working hard most of their life, they will see a turn for the better in middle age and succeed in taking care of their family.

The 27th Day: They will be helpless with lots of troubles. However, the Snake man will have assistance from his wife.

The 28th Day: With both good and bad luck, they will smoothly gain their wealth. They should be mindful of their outspoken personality.

The 29th Day: A hopeless romantic throughout life, they will not accumulate much money.

The 30th Day: They amaze people with their accomplished career. They have lots of wealth and will live a comfortable life.

The Rabbit Curled by the Snake

For expressing filial piety, this is a kind of flour snack popular in the provinces of Shanxi, Shaanxi, and Gansu. Also, in local dialect, "the Rabbit curled by the Snake" sounds like "to be surely rich," denoting people's longing for wealth and a beautiful life.

Overall Fortunes of the Snake Born in Different Hours

11 PM–1 AM: Despite going through lots of hardship, they will not encounter serious adversities and problems and will have a successful career.

1 AM–3 AM: With help from relatives and friends, they enjoy happiness, peace, and a successful career throughout life.

3 AM–5 AM: They are blessed with good luck. Despite the lack of help from relatives, they are strong-willed, courageous, and resourceful when starting from scratch.

5 AM–7 AM: Helped by many friends, they will enjoy a comfortable life. The ups and downs in their career will not matter much.

7 AM–9 AM: Helped both by strangers and parents, they enjoy a smooth career. Throughout their life, they are comfortable and joyful.

9 AM–11 AM: With sharp ups and downs, they never worry about food and clothes in their prime, but will only have a little money left behind in difficult days. They find it hard to have close friends.

11 AM–1 PM: Attracting people of the opposite sex, they are fond of seeking out extramarital affairs and can get support from their lovers in their career development. Despite twists and turns, there will be no serious problems.

1 PM–3 PM: They enjoy very good luck in childhood and in their youth, but there will be many setbacks and troubles in their marriage. They are especially healthy.

3 PM–5 PM: With a smooth career, they are helped by others at every turn and always seem to avert misfortunes. Despite small twists and turns, they lead a comfortable life.

5 PM–7 PM: It will be a bumpy road for the first half of their life. With the help from others, their career will develop rapidly. Their achievements will lead to an influx of wealth.

7 PM–9 PM: With many happy events, they often come across friends of the opposite sex who share the same interests.

They always have success in their career. Despite minor illness and a loss of wealth from time to time, they can turn misfortunes around with the help of benefactors.

9 PM–11 PM: With unfortunate luck, it is better for them to seek career development away from home. They should not tangled with others over trivial things.

Chapter Seven
The Horse

Compare to the other animals in the Chinese zodiac, the Horse holds a special place in the hearts of the Chinese. The Horse is imbued with a masculine spirit that is as vigorous as the Dragon's, making up for the disappointment of the ancient people for the non-existence of a real dragon. Therefore, the Horse replaces the Dragon in the real and perceptive world. The Horse ranks seventh in the Chinese zodiac and it represents romance and enthusiasm.

Lunar Years of the Horse in the Solar Calendar

4 February 1918 to 4 February 1919

4 February 1930 to 4 February 1931

4 February 1942 to 4 February 1943

4 February 1954 to 3 February 1955

4 February 1966 to 3 February 1967

4 February 1978 to 3 February 1979

4 February 1990 to 3 February 1991

4 February 2002 to 3 February 2003

4 February 2014 to 3 February 2015

4 February 2026 to 3 February 2027

4 February 2038 to 3 February 2039

Life Path

People born in the year of the Horse are gifted with strong perception, acute thinking, and physical agility. They are innately resistant in dealing with hardship and highly ambitious with a strong sense of leadership, ingenuity, resourcefulness, activeness, and indomitability. They see things through to the end despite setbacks and often make the impossible seem possible. They make many friends and get along well with other people. Their career luck is just average in their youth, but they will gradually peak after the middle age with many helpful people, which makes it ideal for them to start business. Their career will develop more smoothly if they can have a cooperative partner who is mild-tempered and clear-minded in dealing with things. However, they need to be careful not to give up half way in doing things.

Personality

The Horse is outgoing, romantic, enthusiastic, worships freedom, also unrestrained, independent, frank, optimistic, and articulate. They easily win the trust of friends and subordinates. With strong sense of heroism, they often interfere on behalf of the injured party as well as enjoy praise and worship. However, they are subjective and unwilling to accept suggestions from others, refusing to accept defeat. The Horse is resourceful, acutely insightful, and adaptable in dealing with changes. Very often, they are able to predict what other people fail to think about. Their fault lies in the inability to keep secrets.

Profession

The personality and changeability of the Horse make it unsuitable for them to engage in monotonous jobs. Innately self-confident, they are suitable for doing jobs that give free rein to their talents.

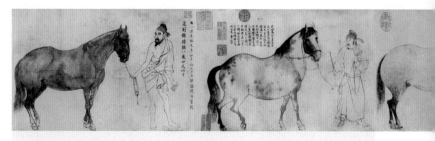

Five Horses

Height: 29.3 cm. Width: 225 cm.
Ink on paper
Beijing Palace Museum.

This is a painting of everlasting fame by Li Gonglin (1049–1106), a painter from the Northern Song Dynasty. The Horse is the animal which is the dearest and closest to mankind. It has been a necessity whether in transportation or in the war. Therefore, running horses can be seen on ancient murals. After the Tang Dynasty, there came into being independent saddled horses in paintings, gradually forming a system of its own. This is a long painting-scroll in five sections. The spirit and texture of horses in this painting are fully featured by single line ink brush, slight light ink, reasonable brush-strokes and nice rhythm, making it the best model for people in the following generation to paint saddled horses with human figures. For this, Li Gonglin is reputed as the "master of sketching."

Love and Marriage

The Horse pays attention to the principles and methods in doing things. With independent views on marriage, they never make careless choices. Once the marriage is decided, they would, as always, treat their spouse with consistent affection. It does not matter if their marriage is not as good as it was imagined at the beginning. The Horse is very responsible and extremely realistic with a slight idealism of sentiments. The Horse is well matched

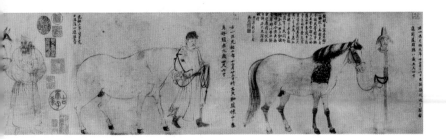

with those born in the year of the Tiger, the Sheep, and the Dog. They should be careful with those of the Rat, the Ox, the Rabbit.

Marriage Compatibility with Women Born in Other Animal Years

The Horse Man with the Rat Woman: They can peacefully co-exist, but they need to avoid making trouble with other people.

The Horse Man with the Ox Woman: The wife will have to be able to bear and make concessions to her husband.

The Horse Man with the Tiger Woman: Both sides are full of energy, pursuing common goals.

The Horse Man with the Rabbit Woman: Both sides will need to be mature in order to experience a deeper, sweeter kind of love.

The Horse Man with the Dragon Woman: This will be a very happy marriage.

The Horse Man with the Snake Woman: Both should respect and love each other.

The Horse Man with the Horse Woman: This will be a happy marriage. The wife will bring warmth and harmony to her family.

The Horse Man with the Sheep Woman: There will be a warm and tender family life if the husband takes good care of his wife.

The Horse Man with the Monkey Woman: They can peacefully co-exist if the marriage is one of true love without ulterior motives.

The Horse Man with the Rooster Woman: This will be a happy marriage if the husband stays close to his wife.

The Horse Man with the Dog Woman: They can peacefully co-exist.

The Horse Man with the Pig Woman: This will be a happy marriage. However, the husband should try not to seek out other women and his wife should change her bad temperament

Marriage Compatibility with Men Born in Other Animal Years

The Horse Woman with the Rat Man: This will be just an average marriage. Both sides tend to be blind with their ideas and impulsive in their actions.

The Horse Woman with the Ox Man: They don't understand each other so it will be difficult for them to live together.

The Horse Woman with the Tiger Man: This will be an ideal marriage. The husband will make sure that his wife's need for independence will not be disregarded.

The Horse Woman with the Rabbit Man: The husband will be a loyal friend to his wife.

The Horse Woman with the Dragon Man: Though everything will go as planned, it will be hard to predict whether their marriage will lasts.

The Horse Woman with Snake Man: This will be a perfect marriage.

The Horse Woman with the Horse Man: This will be a balanced and compatible marriage with devoted children. However, the wife will likely make more concessions to her husband.

The Horse Woman with the Sheep Man: This will be an average marriage though the family will not be the main focus of the husband's attention.

The Horse Woman with the Monkey Man: This will not be a suitable marriage as both tend to manipulate each other's feelings and emotions.

The Horse Woman with the Rooster Man: This will not be a suitable marriage.

The Horse Woman with the Dog Man: This will be a happy marriage. The husband will be absolutely devoted to his wife.

***Galloping Horses* by Xu Beihong**

This painting was completed in 1941. The horse was a hallmark motif of Xu Beihong (1895–1953) in his paintings. His horses appear in various postures full of passion and vigor. Moreover, his galloping horses were painted on the spur of the moment with great passion, producing an amazing force.

The Horse Woman with the Pig Man: This will not be a happy marriage. The husband's need for affection will not be satisfied by his wife. The wife cannot stand the husband's self-consciousness which is too strong.

The Luck of Wealth

People born in the year of the Horse may make a lot of money in business, but also suffer serious loss due to many changes. Therefore, they need to be very, very cautious! The Horse enjoys living luxuriously and showing off. They spend quite a lot of money, so they need to be careful of their "easy come, easy go" mentality, which will lead to little savings.

Overall Fortunes of the Horse
in Different Animal Years

The Year of the Rat: Their luck is quite unfortunate to the extent that they can become the subject of a lawsuit. However, there will be help from others that will shorten this problematic period.

The Year of the Ox: Everything will go as planned—bad luck will turn into opportunities. However, they need to be careful in doing things and seek for peace by being adaptable. It is not advisable for them to engage in gambling and indulge in women.

The Year of the Tiger: They will likely suffer from economic loss, with more adversities and less favorable conditions. However, there will be no serious difficulties. Throughout the year, they need to be conservative and composed. Also, they should be careful who they make friends with so they can stay away from troubles.

The Year of the Rabbit: They will be optimistic. Everything will be smooth and there will be ample wealth. However, they need to be careful in all things and mindful in handling interpersonal relations.

The Year of the Dragon: There will be less favorable conditions and more adversities. They should stick to doing one thing.

The Year of the Snake: They will often suffer from illness, running around tiringly. Whatever they do, it will be disadvantageous. It is advisable for them to do more good deeds, contribute more and ask for less.

The Year of the Horse: They will enjoy career development, have lots of wealth, and get the opportunities for promotion.

The Year of the Sheep: There will be small gains at the beginning of the year and success at the end of the year. However, there will be many obstacles and difficulties throughout the course of the year. They are not supposed to go too far to seek wealth amidst danger. Greed should be checked.

The Year of the Monkey: Whatever they do, there will be success, but also many failures. In general, there will be more favorable conditions and less bad luck.

The Year of the Rooster: There will be success at the beginning of the year. Within the year, there will be several good opportunities which are mostly related to wealth. They should seize these opportunities to develop a business.

The Year of the Dog: There are many ups and downs, but there will surely be achievements as long as they take advantage of opportunities. They should have courage and strength when faced with ups and downs.

The Year of the Pig: It is disadvantageous to seek for wealth. Therefore, they should make friends to acquire more information.

·

Overall Fortunes of the Horse Born in Different Months by the Lunar Calendar

The 1st Lunar Month: They are virtuous, optimistic, outgoing, broad-minded, and knowledgeable. However, their biggest shortcoming is being content very easily and inactive in their career pursuit. They are fond of making friends, always enjoying a comfortable life.

The 2nd Lunar Month: Smart and well-mannered, they pay attention to their appearance. They love freedom and hate the feeling of being restrained. Due to help from relatives, they can tide over hardship and unexpected situations without much problems.

The 3rd Lunar Month: Blessed with good fortune, they are innately smart, knowledgeable, versatile, and ambitious. Thanks to the help from their father and others, they will be free from serious troubles throughout life. They will be successful in whatever they do. They get along well with other people, hence enjoying popularity among them.

The 4th Lunar Month: Working hard all the time, they will make lots of money, but will spend it like water. They have to make their own way without any help from family or relatives. They can be successful in their career if they work out great ambitions against their destiny and stand firm in front of difficulties.

The 5th Lunar Month: They have to make their own way without any help from family or relatives. After going through so much hardship, they will be successful and enjoy a happy life in their old age.

The 6th Lunar Month: They will not have much luck in their early years and will have to work their way up. They will not have their own business until 35 or 36 years old. They will see their life turn around after 40 years old and enjoy a stable life after 50 years old.

The 7th Lunar Month: Smart, intelligent, elegant, attractive, and energetic, they are free from serious troubles throughout life, living in happiness and peace.

The 8th Lunar Month: Smart, talented, immensely wise, and courageous, they don't fear sacrifice. With noble virtue, they are honest and tend to forge profound friendships with others. With their own efforts and help from others, they see gradual development in career and attain achievements. They are free from serious troubles throughout life, enjoying both happiness and longevity.

The 9th Lunar Month: Without any magnificent objectives and ambitions, they stand still and muddle through life even though they are quite talented and intelligent. They will enjoy boundless development if they work hard.

The 10th Lunar Month: Happiness is coupled with hardship throughout life. In their early years, they have no relatives and other people to rely on. Also, they will encounter problems and troubles, hence leading a very hard life. However, they are strong-willed, smart, and capable. After middle age, they are helped by others, resulting in their prosperity later.

The 11th Lunar Month: Righteous and ambitious, they have average luck in their early years but enjoy happiness in old age.

The 12th Lunar Month: Being loyal and devoted to parents, they will enjoy happiness, wealth, and fame far and wide as well as prosperity in their old age. They will live a peaceful life.

Tian Ji and His Horse-Race

Tian Ji often engaged in horse race with other princes of Qi State, gambling with lots of money. Sun Bin found that the strength of their horse-hoofs was pretty much the same. Horses were then divided into three ranks, i.e. the best, the medium and the average. Then, he said to Tian Ji: "I can let you win and all you need to do is to put in a big amount of money." Tian Ji believed and agreed with him, using lots of money to gamble with the king of the Qi State and all other princes. When the horse-race was about to begin, Sun Bin said: "Now, use your average horse to deal with their best horses, use your best horse to deal with their medium horses and use your medium horse to deal with their average horses." With three rounds of race over, Tian Ji lost one and won two, finally gaining lots of money from the king of the Qi State from this gambling. With the same horse but the change of the order of entering the scene, Tian Ji turned the tables.

Overall Fortunes of the Horse Born on Different Days by the Lunar Calendar

The 1st Day: They must try to be strong-willed throughout their life because nothing will be easy. They can only advance if they are persistent.

The 2nd Day: Parents cannot offer help and there will be disputes within the family, leading to many troubles.

The 3rd Day: They are kind, but at the same time they are often misunderstood due to their kindness.

The 4th Day: Despite good luck in dating, they do not have good luck in wealth.

The 5th Day: Versatile and hardworking, they will have fame and wealth at the same time.

The 6th Day: They are mostly close to people with power and wealth. They will have ample money and everlasting good luck.

The 7th Day: They are destined to be lonely. There will not be any hope for official positions, however, there is great prospect for them to develop a business.

The 8th Day: Despite staying away from home and running around, they are helped by others, living a quite comfortable life.

The 9th Day: Smart, ingenious, and highly skilled, they excel in academia and enjoy prosperity.

The 10th Day: Versatile and extensively famous, they enjoy a smooth career with great achievements.

The 11th Day: With no success in their efforts and no relatives to rely on, they have less opportunities and no luck.

The 12th Day: Often suffering from people with ulterior motives and not having solid gains in business, they experience instability throughout life.

The 13th Day: Attractive and honest, they do things with consistency, hence enjoying great trust from other people.

The 14th Day: With good health and a mild temper, they pay attention to etiquette and trustworthiness. They will have an official position and power.

The 15th Day: They are very generous and are fond of apple-polishing others. They go through ups and downs throughout life.

The 16th Day: Innately bold and hot-tempered, they go through ups and downs with both joy and worries throughout life.

The 17th Day: They go through ups and downs in marriage, with more bitterness and less joy in life.

The Marquis Conferred on the Horse

This is an auspicious pattern of Chinese tradition. In Chinese, "monkey" sounds like "marquis," hence resulting in a pun. There were nobilities of five grades in ancient China, with the marquis ranking the second. Here, it refers to officials and nobilities in a general sense. The Monkey on the Horse denotes "at once" in Chinese. This picture means immediate conferment of a marquis or a big official.

The 18th Day: With true power and a firm will, they contribute outstandingly to their community and people. However, they encounter difficulties and failures.

The 19th Day: Smart and outstandingly talented, they will have a successful career and become famous far and wide.

The 20th Day: Destined to have good luck, they have many children, enjoy happiness, longevity, and prosperity in their family and career throughout life.

The 21st Day: They are very popular among people of the opposite sex. However, they accomplish nothing in the end due to a broken life.

The 22nd Day: Experiencing ups and downs throughout life, they will not have devoted children.

The 23rd Day: Being versatile, they can become officials if they try to seek for it and make a fortune if they do business. They encounter minor troubles occasionally which do not constitute danger.

The 24th Day: Men are fond of alcohol and women.

The 25th Day: They will enjoy a successful business and wealth, as well as have friends as benefactors. However, it is a pity that they won't have a harmonious family.

The 26th Day: With both bitterness and joy, they are blessed with an abundant source of wealth and success in business, enjoying prosperity throughout life.

The 27th Day: Working hard throughout life, they will not make a lot of money despite constant small gains. They will live a good life.

The 28th Day: They will probably be in jail more than once, hence caution is required at all times.

The 29th Day: Destined to have good luck, everything will go as they hope for, such as marriage and career.

The 30th Day: Smart, versatile, and attractive, they enjoy a satisfactory marriage, auspiciousness, and peace.

Overall Fortunes of the Horse Born
in Different Hours

11 PM–1 AM: Without help from others, they will suffer from economic loss. However, they will have success if they work hard.

1 AM–3 AM: With help both from family and others, they enjoy a very comfortable life along with rapid career development and lots of wealth. They are outgoing and joyful, free from worries throughout life.

3 AM–5 AM: They are strongly-willed and endurable in face of hardship, single-handedly developing their own career. Despite hardship and difficulties, they will be successful in the end. They live happily in their old age with devoted children.

5 AM–7 AM: With good wealth luck, help from relatives and friendship with many benefactors, they experience a thriving career. However, they may quarrel with others.

7 AM–9 AM: Without help from relatives and others, they will encounter many difficulties in their career development. They need to set goals as early as in childhood and learn a professional skill to their liking.

9 AM–11 AM: They will be engaged in a number of professions and excel in a particular industry. However, they should avoid disputes with others.

11 AM–1 PM: With help from others, they have a happy family and many children without major troubles. However, they are hot-tempered, refusing to listen to the advice of other people.

1 PM–3 PM: They can become high-level officials if they step into politics and they can have endless wealth if they do business, hence enjoying prosperity and wealth throughout life.

3 PM–5 PM: Righteous and stubborn, they do things in an orderly way, being strictly impartial even towards their family members. Despite their high-level official position, they only have a few friends who are noted and powerful people.

5 PM–7 PM: As rich people in a particular area, they enjoy wealth and prosperity in both family life and career. They have

rapid career development thanks to their intelligence and help from others.

7 PM–9 PM: Talented and fond of on-going studying, they can learn new things quickly. They enjoy a very comfortable life with prosperous career. However, they need to be mindful of people with ulterior motives who cause ups and downs for them.

9 PM–11 PM: Out-spoken and capable, they don't bully the kind and fear no evil, but they cannot save money. They have quite undesirable luck in early years, take a turn for the better in the middle age, and live happily in the old age.

Chapter Eight
The Sheep

The Sheep represents beauty and kindness in traditional Chinese views. In ancient times, it was for virtuous people. "The lamb kneels down while sucking his mother's milk" signifies filial piety. Situated in eighth place, the Sheep stands for kindness, beauty, and noble virtues.

Lunar Years of the Sheep in the Solar Calendar

5 February 1919 to 4 February 1920

5 February 1931 to 4 February 1932

5 February 1943 to 4 February 1944

4 February 1955 to 4 February 1956

4 February 1967 to 4 February 1968

4 February 1979 to 4 February 1980

4 February 1991 to 3 February 1992

4 February 2003 to 3 February 2004

4 February 2015 to 3 February 2016

4 February 2027 to 3 February 2028

4 February 2039 to 3 February 2040

Life Path

Those born in the year of the Sheep enjoy very good luck without economic trouble throughout life. They are considerate, stable in doing things, and enterprising. In addition, they get along well with people, sociable, and fond of making friends. They will absolutely lend a hand when seeing others in trouble. They present themselves nobly, hence being very popular among people. They are able to seize opportunities with the help from others to develop their career.

Personality

Mild and sympathetic, they devote themselves to their elders. They are always joyful because they are content with what they have, with characters marked by tenderness in appearance and firmness in mentality. They have strong vitality. However, they are not good at handling adversities and attacks, tending to be pessimistic and timid.

Profession

The Sheep is known for his careful thinking and strong will-power. With a skill unique to them, they find themselves adaptable to do some jobs which require careful thinking, perfect understanding, activeness, and optimism. Also, they find themselves adaptable to do simple and stable jobs. Due to the lack of an adventurous spirit, it is unsuitable for them to engage in a pioneering and highly competitive career.

Love and Marriage

Being responsible, the Sheep take more care of their

spouses than others and show great consideration for their children. Usually, the Sheep woman can accomplish what they wish in love and easily find suitable spouses. The Sheep man can go through ups and downs when it comes to love, hence requiring a sound mastery of their mentality. It is suitable for the Sheep to be matched with those of the Rabbit, the Horse, and the Pig, but they should be careful with those of the Rat, the Ox, and the Dog.

Marriage Compatibility with Women Born in Other Animal Years

The Sheep Man with the Rat Woman: This is not an ideal marriage. Both sides need to make efforts to live a peaceful life.

The Sheep Man with the Ox Woman: Most of them live together peacefully and they can treat each other politely as guests.

The Sheep Man with the Tiger Woman: This will not be a smooth marriage.

The Sheep Man with the Rabbit Woman: They can co-exist together if get along with each other very well, but it lacks profound basis of affection.

The Sheep Man with the Dragon Woman: This will not be a peaceful marriage, as there are always contradictions.

The Sheep Man with the Snake Woman: This will be a perfect marriage which can last forever.

The Sheep Man with the Horse Woman: This will not be a suitable marriage. However, it will be very happy if it is the Sheep woman being matched with the Horse man.

The Sheep Man with the Sheep Woman: This will be a happy marriage.

The Sheep Man with the Monkey Woman: It is difficult for them to be married.

The Sheep Man with the Rooster Woman: They will live together happily.

The Sheep Man with the Dog Woman: They will eventually get married though they will do so reluctantly.

The Sheep Man with the Pig Woman: The marriage will last long if the husband is mild-tempered. Otherwise, it is difficult for them to stay with each other for a lifetime.

Marriage Compatibility with Men Born in Other Animal Years

The Sheep Woman with the Rat Man: They can be married, but they will not feel happy until the husband becomes quite rich.

The Sheep Woman with the Ox Man: This will not be a peaceful marriage, since the husband lacks imagination. He is too realistic and cannot accept the romantic ideas of his wife.

The Sheep Woman with the Tiger Man: Being on very good terms with each other, they often talk and laugh, with happiness and sweetness increasing daily.

The Sheep Woman with the Rabbit Man: This will be a perfect marriage. The husband is fond of the rich imagination of his wife. Both sides are blessed with artistic views, making the marriage more harmonious.

The Sheep Woman with the Dragon Man: This will be quite a nice marriage. However, the wife is not supposed nag at her husband so as to prevent failure of the his career.

The Sheep Woman with the Snake Man: This will be an ideal marriage which will be smooth.

The Sheep Woman with the Horse Man: They will be happy with one another.

The Sheep Woman with the Sheep Man: This will be a happy marriage.

The Sheep Woman with the Monkey Man: They can get married as they have the same interests and desires.

The Sheep Woman with the Rooster Man: Their love is not ideal.

The Sheep Woman with the Dog Man: They keep creating tension between themselves.

The Sheep Woman with the Pig Man: This will be a nice marriage, but the husband will not be able to provide a wealthy life for his wife.

The Luck of Wealth

Those born in the year of the Sheep are economically self-sufficient though they are not billionaires. They live plainly and stably without much trouble. If they concentrate on their career, they will also become great winners starting from scratch.

Overall Fortunes of the Sheep in Different Animal Years

The Year of the Rat: They are on the path of gaining wealth with prosperous business and advanced career. However, they need to be cautious at the end of the year so as to maintain what they have gained.

The Year of the Ox: They experience ups and downs in their fortunes with both opportunities and bad luck. In the middle of the year, nothing goes well and they may have to spend lots of money to eliminate troubles. There are often quarrels and disputes in the family. Everything will be peaceful if they exert forbearance.

The Year of the Tiger: Their fortunes will rise up inevitably, but they should mind people with ulterior motives. They should be courageous and cautious in making friends. Indulgence in women and gambling is not advisable.

The Year of the Rabbit: Their fortunes tend to be associated with wealth with a smooth career. Everything goes quite smoothly, but there will be some setbacks.

The Year of the Dragon: They encounter obstacles in seeking wealth, with their efforts always in vain. Gambling is not advisable since it will land them in a sorry plight.

The Year of the Snake: Every effort results in success and satisfaction.

The Year of the Horse: They enjoy immense opportunities and benefits.

The Year of the Sheep: The whole year can be peaceful if they are cautious and careful in making plans at all times.

Four Goats

Height: 22.5 cm. Width: 24 cm.
Light color on thin silk
Beijing Palace Museum

This is a painting by Chen Juzhong, a painter from the Southern Song Dynasty. In a structure of a substantial scene on the left and an elusive scene on the right, it depicts four goats with fur of different colors. The painting is marked by simple structure, succinct brushwork and tender color in sharp contrast, fully revealing the naughty and war-like instinct of goats. The slope is covered with withered trees and thorns as well as grass, showing an atmosphere of serenity and wilderness in clear autumn with strong appeal of life.

The Year of the Monkey: Though all things are to their satisfaction, they are not supposed to get carried away by their success and ask for too much.

The Year of the Rooster: They can gain wealth frequently if they work away from home. However, they should not go too far since there are more bad luck and less opportunities in this year. Also, they should be cautious with their relatives and friends in dealing with wealth.

The Year of the Dog: Taking defense as offense, they should be cautious in everything.

The Year of the Pig: There is no hope of becoming an official, in addition to failure in making friends and difficulties in doing business. Worse still, they will not be in good health. Therefore, they are advised not to take risks and they should be cautious in everything.

Overall Fortunes of the Sheep Born in Different Months by the Lunar Calendar

The 1st Lunar Month: Serene, elegant, bright, and lively, they are extremely talented. However, they have to make their own way since they don't have family and relatives to rely on.

The 2nd Lunar Month: With a mild personality, they are very good at socializing with people in a flexible and popular manner. Living a comfortable life, they are helped by friends and others and supported by parents and brothers, hence enjoying benefits in all things.

The 3rd Lunar Month: Bright and smart with noble virtues and an outgoing personality, they are in good health and on good terms with other people. Also, they are helped by family members and supported by friends and others, enjoying happiness and peace without serious troubles, but with fame and gains.

The 4th Lunar Month: Despite frequent troubles, they are blessed with happiness in their old age. They work hard in early years, but enjoy happiness in middle age and old age. In spite of ups and downs in their career, they can overcome all difficulties and progress.

The 5th Lunar Month: They are in a position of leading hundreds of thousands of people, receiving admiration and support. Also, they have a brilliant career without serious troubles in life. However, they are marked by rudeness and hot temper.

The 6th Lunar Month: Warm-hearted, faithful, and righteous, they enjoy both fame and gains. Also, they can do everything at will, live in peace with others, never cheat but help people whole-heartedly. As a result, they have a prosperous family and an endless source of wealth.

The 7th Lunar Month: Going through sharp ups and downs in life, they can stand up with tenacious efforts in hardship. Also, they are marked by wisdom and courage, a firm will, and a down-to-earth personality, hence deserving respect.

The 8th Lunar Month: Bright and wise, they are extremely naughty and perform poorly in school during childhood. They will make remarkable progress at school after ten years old until they become extensively famous. They will encounter small problems that can easily be eliminated.

The 9th Lunar Month: Despite being well-educated, they are poorly grounded and encounter hardship in starting a business. They work hard throughout life and suffer from illness continuously. Their life will be peaceful if they seek for stability as the top priority and success as the second priority.

The 10th Lunar Month: Bright, ingenious, and exceedingly wise, they are helped by others, getting a remarkable official position, respect, happiness, and gains throughout life.

The 11th Lunar Month: Despite a comfortable life, they don't live outstandingly, with just an average career. They begin to see light in their development in middle age after going through lots of obstacles.

The 12th Lunar Month: Honest and kind, they are loyal and devoted to their elders. However, they are not duly repaid despite their help to others. Working hard throughout life, they enjoy happiness in their old age.

Three Sheep Bringing the Advent of Spring and Prosperity (*San Yang Kai Tai*)

This is an auspicious pattern of Chinese tradition. Three sheep eating grass under warm sunlight stands for the advent of spring, renewal of everything, prosperity, and a smooth path to all things. The sun (*yang*) sounds exactly like the Sheep (*yang*). Literally speaking, it would be more direct to explain that *san yang* refers to three suns, i.e. the early sun, the mid-sun, and the late sun. The Sheep is also concerned with auspiciousness (*xiang*). According to folk customs, "auspiciousness" is mostly written as "auspicious sheep." *Kai tai* stands for lots of sources of wealth.

Overall Fortunes of the Sheep Born
on Different Days by the Lunar Calendar

The 1st Day: They may encounter obstacles. However, enterprising and indomitable, they are good at applying wisdom and advancing against difficulties.

The 2nd Day: Without good luck in their early years, they work hard with more failure than success. However, they will have success after the middle age.

The 3rd Day: They go through lots of ups and downs in life. They will be put in jail if they act with bad motives.

The 4th Day: With a smooth career, they live light-heartedly.

The 5th Day: With both joy and worry, they live quite comfortably in their early years. They work hard in their young age and begin to enjoy good luck in middle age. However, they still encounter problems in career development.

The 6th Day: Attractive and enterprising, they are likely to have success and they enjoy fairly good luck in their middle age and old age.

The 7th Day: Mild and lenient, they get along well with others, enjoy a good reputation, and live in harmony with neighbors. Also, they are blessed with fairly good luck in wealth.

The 8th Day: Innately stubborn and sentimental in doing things, the man is marked by a very strong self-respect. On the contrary, the woman is innately mild and agreeable with others.

The 9th Day: With average intelligence, they are not so enterprising and sometimes not in good health. With undesirable fortunes in their early years, their luck will take a turn for the better in later years.

The 10th Day: With outstanding wisdom, they are excellent students. What they do will surely be to their satisfaction if they keep working hard.

The 11th Day: They tend to take action for others against injustice and readily help others, hence receiving respect.

The 12th Day: Ambitious and talented, they will be leaders in their community. After middle age, they will reach their peak, with a prosperous family and career.

The 13th Day: They have outstanding artistic and cultural talents, making achievements and winning glory throughout life. The woman will be luckier than the man.

The 14th Day: Working hard and going through lots of ups and downs in their early years, they will see a turn for the better in middle age.

The 15th Day: With both opportunities and bad luck, they have power and influence, but find it easy to have enemies and go through ups and downs.

The 16th Day: Bright and rational, with a strong sense of judgment, they are conceited with few friends, hence living an average life.

The 17th Day: With outstanding intelligence and noble virtue and reputation, they enjoy fame and gains throughout life.

The 18th Day: With an unpredictable personality, they are versatile but not well-versed in any of them. They experience many changes in life. The woman is virtuous and kind-hearted.

The 19th Day: Being fond of vanity, they are wealthy in appearance, but visionary in mentality. The woman is down-to-earth, honest, and outgoing.

The 20th Day: The man is bright and the woman is kind-hearted. They are enterprising, loyal to their friends, and grateful to what they have been given.

The 21st Day: Despite true talents, they find no place to display them, hence complaining about their environment and other people.

The 22nd Day: Because of undesirable luck, they have no one to go to. After getting through a difficult period, they will enjoy unexpected good luck.

The 23rd Day: Because of undesirable luck, they are likely to suffer from seriously difficult time. This can be turned into an opportunity if they can get through this trouble period.

The 24th Day: They will enjoy blessings from their ancestors. Also, they tend to become officials with the help and promotion from others.

The 25th Day: With outstanding talents, they are very flexible in doing things and dealing with people. Also, they are known to uphold justice and are selfless.

The 26th Day: With both joy and worry, they go through ups and downs. The career is smooth, though there will be troubles with their family.

The 27th Day: Without exerting restraints on their behaviors, they live a colorful life and enjoy smoking and wine. They live quite comfortably though they cannot make a lot of money.

The 28th Day: Energetic and intelligent, they are resolute and strong-willed in doing things. They are able to start a business with their own efforts.

The 29th Day: They devote all their efforts in prospering their family. Despite average luck in their early years, they can start a business after middle age and may become a very rich person.

The 30th Day: Endowed with immense opportunities, they work light-heartedly with lots of influx of wealth. They come from wealthy and influential family background.

Overall Fortunes of the Sheep Born in Different Hours

11 PM–1 AM: Despite quite many ups and downs in their life, they are helped by others without serious troubles.

1 AM–3 AM: With noble virtues, talents, and righteousness, they get along very well with other people. They will have success if they make unremitting efforts.

3 AM–5 AM: They enjoy good luck throughout life. Despite various unfortunate incidents, they can overcome them. They are blessed with accomplishments in their career and increasing reputation as well as good luck in wealth, which are all attributed to their own efforts.

5 AM–7 AM: Bright, spirited, and strong-willed, they are

not afraid of hardship and engage in career at the risk of their life. Also, they are helped by friends and others, hence enjoying prosperous career development, attaining fame and achievements. However, they should be cautious of complete failure

7 AM 9 AM: They will develop their career far away from home. However, their career is not so remarkable and their wealth is not so great. Thanks to the help from friends and others, their career proceeds quite smoothly.

9 AM–11 AM: Working hard from place to place, they are lucky to be helped by others, but their career is not so remarkable. They will encounter lots of danger, but they are able to overcome them.

11 AM–1 PM: They can receive help from family and others, hence being able to make achievements in their career. Broad-minded, they are not particular about details. Despite some minor illness, they mostly enjoy longevity.

1 PM–3 PM: Bright and smart with overwhelming talent, they are fond of learning new things. Also, they are honest, kind, and ready to help others. They encounter quite many ups and downs with both joy and worry. In their early years, their career may have problems, but they have quite nice life in their middle age and old age.

3 PM–5 PM: They enjoy unhindered success in everything and quite a rich source of wealth. However, they will not have a satisfactory spouse.

5 PM–7 PM: Versatile, ingenious, and flexible, they can have success in their career if they stay away from home. They fail to become wealthy in their early years, but enjoy a smooth road in middle age, as well as happiness and longevity in old age.

7 PM–9 PM: They won't have good luck in their early years, but enjoy development in middle age and happiness in old age. They may go through ups and downs in marriage, hence requiring caution.

9 PM–11 PM: They will not have help from family. They make mistakes in making friends and they are often troubled by people with ulterior motives. They often quarrel with others.

Chapter Nine
The Monkey

To the people in ancient times, the Monkey is synonymous for "waiting." In other words, the Monkey is innately bright and alert, able to identify the hunter's bait. Instead of going straight for the food, it waits and observes for a long time before taking action, making sure that there is no ambush. The Monkey, ranking ninth in the Chinese zodiac, represents "flexibility and intelligence."

Lunar Years of the Monkey in the Solar Calendar

5 February 1920 to 3 February 1921

5 February 1932 to 3 February 1933

5 February 1944 to 3 February 1945

5 February 1956 to 3 February 1957

5 February 1968 to 3 February 1969

5 February 1980 to 3 February 1981

4 February 1992 to 3 February 1993

4 February 2004 to 3 February 2005

4 February 2016 to 2 February 2017

4 February 2028 to 2 February 2029

4 February 2040 to 2 February 2041

Life Path

Those born in the year of the Monkey are highly intelligent, competitive, and wise in sociability, plus in tacit agreement with mankind and a sense of brotherhood. They are energetic, robust, optimistic, smart, courageous, and very adaptable to the change of the environment with a strong enterprising spirit and innate indomitability. Also, they are very eager to learn and well-read with amazing memory, intellectual flexibility, great creativity, and expertise in seizing opportunities for further development and a favorable situation. They should cultivate patience and will-power so as to avoid the defect of rashness in action.

Personality

The Monkey is marked by liveliness, activeness, agility, quick reaction, superb intelligence, adaptability in doing things, good capability of solving problems, and a strong desire to show off. They are apt to be conceited, in addition to disregarding all rules and regulations, hence causing unnecessary loss.

Profession

The Monkey enjoys a stable and smooth career. Fond of seeking for new things, they dislike being controlled. They are well-versed in verbal expression with an extremely strong desire to show-off, which is suitable for them to start a business or develop new business. However, they are not patient enough, hence they require careful planning, realism, devoted operation in order to get progress in steady advancement.

Love and Marriage

The Monkey enjoys a peaceful family and pays special attention to kinship with an instinctive devotion to parents. Pampering children might be their weakness. They value marriage and love each other for a lasting relationship. However, they tend to hope that their wife would follow their ideas. It is suitable for those of the Monkey to be matched with those of the Rat and the Dragon, but they need to be careful in matching with those of the Tiger, the Pig, and the Snake.

Marriage Compatibility with Women Born in Other Animal Years

The Monkey Man with the Rat Woman: It will be a perfect marriage. They love each other and will enjoy sweetness, warmth, and tenderness forever.

The Monkey Man with the Ox Woman: This is quite a peaceful marriage. The wife loves her husband very much. The smart husband will do a good job handling family disagreements, bringing joy to life.

The Monkey Man with the Tiger Woman: This will not be an ideal marriage. The action and ideas of the husband disappoints his wife very much and she occasionally seeks for consolation with other men, hence resulting in disputes.

The Monkey Man with the Rabbit Woman: A happy family can be established, but the husband sometimes has some wrong ideas. Therefore, the wife must exert restraint over her husband.

The Monkey Man with the Dragon Woman: They can live together. The husband is attractive to the wife. Though he is sometimes disappointed, he will not let his wife know it.

The Monkey Man with the Snake Woman: Despite some disharmony between them, if the husband is fond of his wife with appropriate adjustment, they can also establish a happy family, which requires favorable conditions in all aspects.

The Monkey Man with the Horse Woman: This will not be an

Monkey King

This is a character in *Journey to the West*, one of the four noted novels in China, and related legends. The Monkey King, born in an immortal rock, is said to excel in 72 changes. On the way to India, he escorted Monk Tangseng to seek the Buddhist scripts as his sacred mission. All the way, he fought to subdue ghosts and evils and experienced 81 difficulties, finally helping Monk Tangseng to obtain the genuine Buddhist scripts and attain success in practicing Buddhism. For this, he was conferred as the Invincible Buddha. The success of *Journey to the West* lies in the creation of Monkey King.

ideal marriage. The husband will disappoint his wife, who needs a healthy kind love.

The Monkey Man with the Sheep Woman: They can live together since the wife can arouse the interest of her husband. However, the husband must be wealthy.

The Monkey Man with the Monkey Woman: This is quite a suitable marriage. They can work together to do the right thing which will please them and further consolidate their marriage.

The Monkey Man with the Rooster Woman: It will almost be impossible.

The Monkey Man with the Dog Woman: It will not be easy for them to get along with each other.

The Monkey Man with the Pig Woman: Despite some disharmony between them, they can get married, on condition that they love each other in order to share a stable life.

Marriage Compatibility with Men Born in Other Animal Years

The Monkey Woman with the Rat Man: They can live together joyfully.

The Monkey Woman with the Ox Man: They can live together. The husband loves his wife very much and is willing to make lots of sacrifice for and concession to her.

The Monkey Woman with the Tiger Man: It is not easy for them to get along with each other. If the husband stays far away from home, his wife knows how to get him to return home.

The Monkey Woman with the Rabbit Man: This will be a very happy marriage. Both sides enjoy a tacit agreement and feel the need to be together.

The Monkey Woman with the Dragon Man: This will be a perfect marriage. The husband can protect his wife while she can offer lots of beneficial opinions and advice to her self-confident husband.

The Monkey Woman with the Snake Man: It will be better for them not to live together, since both sides often play tricks, hence leading to contradiction between them.

The Monkey Woman with the Horse Man: It will be difficult for them to get to know each other, hence resulting in a short-lived relationship.

The Monkey Woman with the Sheep Man: It will be almost impossible for them to live together.

The Monkey Woman with the Monkey Man: They can live together and they will cooperate to do right things.

The Monkey Woman with the Rooster Man: There is no tacit agreement between them. The wife can benefit a lot from her husband but she would still not be satisfied, hence always leading to displeasure.

The Monkey Woman with the Dog Man: They can get along with each other and pay attention to reality together.

The Monkey Woman with the Pig Man: There is a possibility of establishing a family as long as the wife is fond of her talented husband. Moreover, this will be a happy marriage through coordination.

The Luck of Wealth

Those born in the year of the Monkey have prosperous luck of wealth and an increase of income by a big margin. However, they should mind troubles caused by such luck of wealth. They should quickly identify the traps in their economic contact with other people as well as economic contact with relatives and friends.

Overall Fortunes of the Monkey in Different Animal Years

The Year of the Rat: They are marked by prosperous business operation, ample wealth, noble positions, help from others, lucky in everything, and an extensive freedom of action.

Monkeys Scoop Up the Moon from the Well

Once upon a time, 500 monkeys wandered in the forest and came to a big tree. Under the tree, there was a well with the moon reflected in it. Seeing the shadow of the moon, the leader of the band of monkeys said: "The moon will be drowned today since it has fallen into the well. We should scoop it up so as to bring light to the long night in the world." They discussed about how to scoop it up. At this moment, the leader of the monkeys said: "I know how to scoop it up. I get hold of a tree branch while you grasp my tail. Then, we can scoop it up with many hands and feet in connection." Therefore, all the monkeys did according to what their leader advised. Suddenly, the tree branch was broken and all the monkeys fell into the well. Now, people often use this allusion as admonishment, i.e. there will surely be trouble if one troubles oneself over unnecessary fuss.

The Year of the Ox: Working in other places would bring them a smooth life. They need to be careful about the supply of clothing and food if they stay in their hometown.

The Year of the Tiger: With both opportunities and bad luck, ups and downs, they are apt to encounter disputes in marriage which will hurt them both physically and mentally in addition to economic loss. They should be careful about safety when going out for employment.

The Year of the Rabbit: They gain a lot through business operation. Difficulties do not matter much to them.

The Year of the Dragon: They enjoy a smooth flow of good luck when it comes to wealth. Their efforts of many years will produce results. However, they should be careful about people with ulterior motives.

They Year of the Snake: They are apt to suffer from serious illness, even to the extent of being confined in bed. As luck would have it, timely medical treatment will turn the danger into safety.

The Year of the Horse: They enjoy a smooth flow of luck with lots of happy tidings in the family. They attain gains through investment. Their luck of wealth is extremely good and they have income from many sources. However, they should not be too greedy

The Year of the Sheep: They will make some achievements in career and gain desirably in their investment. However, they should be cautious of being cheated.

The Year of the Monkey: They are involved with lots of romance, but without good luck of wealth. Too much romance will hurt them easily.

The Year of the Rooster: They have access to fame, career success, and luck of wealth through efforts. However, too much attention to romance is apt to be disadvantageous to their love and marriage, causing both physical and mental exhaustion.

The Year of the Dog: Their career and luck of wealth are not ideal and even their past good luck will be exhausted. Therefore, they need to be cautious in seeking for good luck through gradual restoration of vigor and vitality.

The Year of the Pig: They encounter endless lawsuits due to troubles caused by people with ulterior motives, hence leading to undesirable career and the lack of luck of wealth. However, they will overcome difficulties with the help of others.

Overall Fortunes of the Monkey Born in Different Months by the Lunar Calendar

The 1st Lunar Month: With lots of energy, they go out to seek for employment with many good prospects. However, they suffer from some minor illness.

The 2nd Lunar Month: They encounter troubles one after another with bad luck while seeking for official position and wealth, being apt to lose both fame and gain.

The 3rd Lunar Month: With superb talents, they enjoy a

happy marriage. Also, all their adversities and bad luck can be turned into favorable conditions and opportunities, leading to a bright future.

The 4th Lunar Month: Working hard all the time, they are knowledgeable, talented, and famous, enjoying prosperity and glory throughout life.

The 5th Lunar Month: Being polite and courteous in getting along with people and handling things, they count on their own efforts to achieve success in everything.

The 6th Lunar Month: With both opportunities and bad luck, they enjoy a free and perfect marriage together with devoted children.

The 7th Lunar Month: They live peacefully and freely throughout life since they are able to achieve what they work for.

The 8th Lunar Month: They will make great accomplishments, enjoy endless happiness and prosperity or immense fame in addition to a peaceful family.

The 9th Lunar Month: Despite being talented and enterprising, they will encounter frustrations and failures. They will live an ordinary life.

The 10th Lunar Month: They will live in an ordinary family without remarkable achievements. They will suffer from bad luck if they do things beyond their reach.

The 11th Lunar Month: With ups and downs in a low spirit, they will seldom think about making progress.

The 12th Lunar Month: With ups and downs and without much planning, their career will proceed undesirably, but they will enjoy peace in their old age.

Overall Fortunes of the Monkey Born on Different Days by the Lunar Calendar

The 1st Day: Blessed with opportunities, they are willing to serve others. The man is talented while the woman is virtuous and versatile.

The 2nd Day: With both opportunities and bad luck, they will often encounter several unfortunate events at the same time. Therefore, they should be careful in avoiding adversities while trying to gain favorable conditions, but they should not do it against the laws of action.

The 3rd Day: They will enjoy fame and success in the first half of their life. They should be cautious as they are apt to lose all they have gained in the second half of their life.

The 4th Day: They will enjoy very good luck and lots of wealth in their early years, but suffer from bad luck in their old age. Therefore, they should set aside savings for a rainy day.

The 5th Day: Bright, able, vigorous, and flexible in handling things, they are blessed with lots of good luck.

The 6th Day: They seek for career development through twists and turns, and for wealth through hard work to make ends meet. They enjoy happiness in the second half of their life.

The 7th Day: Despite working at many posts, they make little success. They go through lots of ups and downs as well as twists and turns. In spite of going all out, they find it difficult to be successful.

The 8th Day: Working hard throughout life, they have access to fame and gains, enjoy happiness and wealth, and be in a prestigious position.

The 9th Day: Flexible, strong-willed, and very enterprising, they are persistent when doing things, hence making it suitable for them to have their own business.

The 10th Day: They are outgoing, composed, and righteous, doing things in a genuine manner.

The 11th Day: They enjoy a smooth career and ample wealth, but may suffer from discord in their marriage.

The 12th Day: Despite peaceful life, they fail to accomplish remarkably in their career. Their luck of wealth is average and their marriage is not a good one.

The 13th Day: Working hard in their early years, they will see a turn for the better after thirty years old. They have good luck and are helped by others when it comes to gaining prestigious position.

The White Ape Steals Peaches

As legend goes, in the Warring States Period (475–221 BC), there was a family in the mountain, with the mother and the son living together. The son was covered with white hair, looking like an ape. For this, the mother named him Xiaobai (Little White).

The mother suddenly fell ill one day, having to stay in bed. One night, the dying mother saw an old immortal come and handed over a bright red peach to her, saying: "This is an immortal peach presented by the Queen Mother. You will be cured if you eat it up!" She took it and had two bites reluctantly, feeling good all over at once. While being joyful, she woke up with a start, sensing that she had a dream! The next day, she told her son about the dream. Xiaobai could not help shouting repeatedly: "My mother's illness can be cured!" As it turned out, he met an old man yesterday while gathering firewood. The old man told him that the Queen Mother had two peach gardens specially for a grand peach meeting. Since his mother was instructed by the old man in her dream related to the cure of illness by eating the peach, he should try to get the peach to extricate his mother from her illness.

Xiaobai trekked day and night across mountains and rivers through so much hardship. Finally, he got to the peach garden and brought the peach home. After eating three immortal peaches, Xiaobai's mother had her illness cured three days later.

The 14th Day: Blessed with ancestral wealth and educated parents, they will be helped often by others, hence enjoying prosperity throughout life.

The 15th Day: Mild, honest, kind, and respectful, they are blessed with lots of success to their satisfaction despite many ups and downs.

The 16th Day: Bright, rational, and composed, they will have a prestigious position and a satisfactory marriage.

The 17th Day: They are innately smart and versatile. Despite difficulties in making big money, they will make small amounts continuously. They will live a decent life.

The 18th Day: Despite hard work in the first half of their life, they will live a stable life with enough wealth. However, they may suffer from illness in the second half of their life.

The 19th Day: Knowledgeable and talented with a prestigious position, they will go through many twists and turns.

The 20th Day: The man will lack will-power and fails consistently, constantly changing professions and residences. There will also be an undesirable marriage.

The 21st Day: They may seem like lucky people, but they will suffer from the decline of luck and live an ordinary life. For the man, the decline will be due to his indulgence in wine and women.

The 22nd Day: With sweetness coming after bitterness, they will go through many troubles, ups and downs, and hardships in their early years. There will be a turn for the better after middle age.

The 23rd Day: Being very versatile, the man will not have to work too hard since he will enjoy wealth and influence.

The 24th Day: Without help from parents and friends, they will aim at objectives beyond their reach, hence living an ordinary life.

The 25th Day: Being fond of reading, the man is talented while the woman is pretty. They can make great accomplishments thanks to the help from others.

The 26th Day: The man is bright and there is a lot he can do in terms of seeking for employment and doing business. They will be wealthy after middle age. The woman is smart and beautiful.

The 27th Day: The man has talents and immense resourcefulness with the ability to accomplish a lot. They will have access to many sources of wealth, but spend money like water, hence being unable to save money.

The 28th Day: Having extraordinary ability of leadership, they will enjoy prestigious positions, fame, and success.

The 29th Day: Despite adversities for a time and frequent lawsuits, they will see a turn for the better after 18 years old, without illness and troubles.

The 30th Day: The man will have a desirable family and career. They will have more successes than failures. They earn ample wealth. However, for the man, he will be apt to focus on women while ignoring friends.

Overall Fortunes of the Monkey Born in Different Hours

11 PM–1 AM: Despite a prosperous career, they are apt to encounter people with ulterior motives. Interference from people

with ulterior motives will lead to their poor luck of getting a prestigious position as well as average luck in their career and wealth.

1 AM–3 AM: With help from others, they will get twice the result with half of their efforts.

3 AM–5 AM: In a low position, they always fail to realize their aspiration with average career development and luck of wealth.

5 AM–7 AM: Being apt to suffer from troubles, they will always helped by others, turning bad luck into opportunities.

7 AM–9 AM: Despite superb talents, intelligence, and great capability, they have many strong opponents, making it easy to step on the toes of other people.

9 AM–11 AM: Despite continuous troubles throughout life, they are helped by many people, thus being able to avoid adversities while pursuing their goals.

11 AM–1 PM: They live as common folks due to undesirable trends of luck and failure to realize their aspirations.

1 PM–3 PM: Despite desirable career and luck of wealth, they will not be in good health or in a desirable marriage.

3 PM–5 PM: They will be joyful throughout life. However, such joy is not substantial since they will be troubled by many people with ulterior motives.

5 PM–7 PM: Refusing to stay still innately, they travel around the country for pleasure. However, they will live an ordinary life with undesirable destiny.

7 PM–9 PM: It is difficult for them to make their dreams come true. Their luck in career and wealth is undesirable. However, they will enjoy a nice marriage.

9 PM–11 PM: With the help from others throughout life, they will be able to accomplish many things through lots of efforts, thus enjoying a bright future.

Chapter Ten
The Rooster

The Rooster is the only bird among the twelve animal signs. As the legend goes, a beautiful golden rooster lived in the sun, triggering off the rise of the sun from the east in early morning. His ancestors were the three-footed bird, the fire-bird, and the phoenix. As the symbol of heralding in and celebrating joyful news, the Rooster represents great socialness and ranks tenth in the Chinese zodiac.

Lunar Years of the Rooster in the Solar Calendar

4 February 1921 to 3 February 1922

4 February 1933 to 3 February 1934

4 February 1945 to 3 February 1946

4 February 1957 to 3 February 1958

4 February 1969 to 3 February 1970

4 February 1981 to 3 February 1982

4 February 1993 to 3 February 1994

4 February 2005 to 3 February 2006

3 February 2017 to 3 February 2018

3 February 2029 to 3 February 2030

3 February 2041 to 3 February 2042

Life Path

Those born in the year of the Rooster are lucky to be praised by others. With great ambition and resourcefulness, they usually possess more foresight in everything when compared with all others, clearly aware of the trend of future development, so they are well-planned in doing things. In addition to often having novel ideas, they handle things with great ability and thoughtfulness. The Rooster is intelligent, smart, social, and capable of reading the minds of others. With acute reaction, they can immediately think of related measures to deal with whatever comes up. As experts of social graces, they are optimistic in handling things. They can be people of mild and cordial personality. They can also become people with ulterior motives and shrewd tricks. They need to pay attention to the feelings and dignity of others as well as prevent themselves from being completely self-centered in terms of interest.

Personality

The Rooster is frank, active, resourceful, exclusively dedicated, hardworking, enthusiastic, and generous. They are marked by eagerness to win over all others, high concentration, quick reaction, a sense of responsibility, strict observance of disciplines, and disgust at loafers. However, they are featured by a strong sense of vanity, indulgence in pleasure, and are big show-offs.

Profession

With great ambition, the Rooster does not care about loss and gain. They are resourceful and able to probe into the focus of things. With a strong focus and will-power, they tend to indomitably carry on with things that average people are apt to feel tired of. However, they cannot bear engaging in dull and monotonous professions. They like to do work that gives them a sense of fulfilment.

Love and Marriage

With healthy self-respect, they feel disgusted when they have to rely on others. They are apt to be induced by people of the opposite sex and are truly devoted to them. Once married, they would value family. It is suitable for those of the Rooster to be matched with those of the Ox, the Dragon, and the Snake. They should be cautious of being matched with those of the Rat, the Rabbit, the Rooster and the Dog.

Marriage Compatibility with Women Born in Other Animal Years

The Rooster Man with the Rat Woman: Their affection will not be affected even if they quarrel occasionally.

The Rooster Man with the Ox Woman: This will be a happy marriage. However, the husband must exert restraint on what he says and what he does.

The Rooster Man with the Tiger Woman: Their marriage will not be ideal or the most perfect.

The Rooster Man with the Rabbit Woman: This will be a mild, peaceful, and average marriage. There will be both sons and daughters.

The Rooster Man with the Dragon Woman: Coordination is required between them, but the husband will pay considerable attention to the career and position of his wife.

The Rooster Man with the Snake Woman: This will be quite a balanced marriage, since both will be good at safeguarding their reputation, hence resulting in less clashes.

The Rooster Man with the Horse Woman: Despite displeasure occasionally, their marriage will be quite nice.

The Rooster Man with the Sheep Woman: This will be a peaceful marriage which requires concerted efforts to maintain it.

The Rooster Man with the Monkey Woman: This will not be an ideal marriage. The wife will never be content with what is given by her husband.

The Rooster Man with the Rooster Woman: This will be a good marriage if both sides can manage well, otherwise it cannot last long.

The Rooster Man with the Dog Woman: Despite quarrels, they will still enjoy quite a nice marriage.

The Rooster Man with the Pig Woman: This will be quite a reluctant marriage since what the husband says and does makes his wife feel disgusted.

Marriage Compatibility with Men Born in Other Animal Years

The Rooster Woman with the Rat Man: They will live together peacefully. There will be some quarrels. Both sides need to compromise with each other.

The Rooster Woman with the Ox Man: This will be a happy marriage. Both sides will realize their self-values in a peaceful life.

The Rooster Woman with the Tiger Man: It will likely be a happy marriage. The key lies in forbearance and inclusiveness.

The Rooster Woman with the Rabbit Man: Their relationship will be average, but they will hold on to their wealth and marriage. Their children will be very promising in their future careers.

The Rooster Woman with the Dragon Man: Their relationship is not so good, but their family will be happy if both sides make concerted efforts.

The Rooster Woman with the Snake Man: This will be a perfect marriage. They will often discuss the philosophy of life and appreciate each other.

The Rooster Woman with the Horse Man: There will be some ups and downs in their marriage. They will be able to help each other and live to the end of their lives.

The Rooster Woman with the Sheep Man: This will not be a

The Virtuous Rooster

Height: 173.5 cm. Width: 95.5 cm.
Color on paper

This is a painting by Li Shan (1686–1762), a painter in the Qing Dynasty. The Rooster is a common motif in the field of flower-bird paintings. It was endowed by ancient people with five virtues, regarding it as a virtuous animal. The comb of the Rooster and the cockscomb flower sound like *guan* (official). Therefore, it is very popular since it is usually regarded as being an official or a higher official. Big characters unique to the painter were written on the upper part of the painting, constituting a compressed space together with the flower and the rock of the same roughness and weight at the lower part. The rooster at the center overlooks and turns its head, seeming to have endless energy to burst out. The appeal of the painting is well expressed in such a tense confrontation.

very ideal marriage. The husband will not understand the spiritual world of his wife.

The Rooster Woman with the Monkey Man: Since there are big differences between them, marriage will be difficult for them.

The Rooster Woman with the Rooster Man: They admire each other's talents and will be able to satisfy one another. Both need compromise with each other in order to have a nice marriage.

The Rooster Woman with the Dog Man: There will be quarrels. Such a situation may change if freedom is available between them.

The Rooster Woman with the Pig Man: The marriage will continue if forbearance and inclusiveness are exerted. Otherwise, there will be more bad luck.

The Luck of Wealth

The Rooster enjoys quite good luck when it comes to wealth. To say the least, they don't have to worry about daily necessities. Despite the lack of money in their young age, they will gradually see a turn for the better in middle age. Through their own efforts, they will have their own business or get the jobs they desire.

Overall Fortunes of the Rooster in Different Animal Years

The Year of the Rat: They will suffer from economic loss at the beginning of the year and make up for it at the end of the year. In the second half of the year, they should seize the opportunity to make more progress, hence having small gains.

The Year of the Ox: Despite ups and downs, they will have opportunities to become outstanding people.

The Year of the Tiger: They will enjoy a prosperous business and a rich source of wealth. Minor illnesses will not matter much.

The Year of the Rabbit: They should not think about striking luck by fluke and never do business with others. Starting a business through hard work can surely bring peace and wealth to them.

The Year of the Dragon: With a lot of power in hand, they will make amazing success at one go. However, they need to be more careful.

The Year of the Snake: There will be fame but without gains, though they won't have to worry about daily necessities. For them, there will be less bad luck and more opportunities. They will have success at the end of the year.

The Year of the Horse: With both bad luck and opportunities, they will go through sharp ups and downs. Though sometimes they will encounter sudden troubles, happy tidings will also be continuous.

The Year of the Sheep: With a smooth path to a desirable career development, they will enjoy good luck at the beginning of the year and should mind their actions at the end of the year.

The Year of the Monkey: There will be a sharp drop of luck

with no benefit from starting a business. Moreover, there will be obstacles in their efforts for progress, in addition to undesirable mind and health. They should be conservative and calm and try to avoid staying far away from home.

The Year of the Rooster: The plan for starting a business will not be a smooth one. There will be small gains at the end of the year.

The Year of the Dog: They will be promoted if encountering helpful people, getting twice the results with half of their efforts. However, they should be cautious while seeking for fame in other places. Otherwise, their opportunities will be coupled with bad luck, resulting in more troubles.

The Year of the Pig: There will not be many opportunities, including the pursuit for wealth. They need to be careful while staying away from home. Their work situation will be average. They should be careful in every aspect.

Overall Fortunes of the Rooster Born in Different Months by the Lunar Calendar

The 1st Lunar Month: While they will live a comfortable life, they have to rely on themselves when it comes to their career. Most of them will enjoy longevity with good health.

The 2nd Lunar Month: Bright, smart, and knowledgeable, they fail to have good opportunities. It will not be until middle and old age that their learning can be applied to practice. With an introverted personality, they will not get along much with people.

The 3rd Lunar Month: Innately intelligent, they are specially fond of study, possessing very good academic knowledge, and have the luck of being in an official position. Being adaptable to any situation, they follow the tide of social development closely, hence enjoying a smooth career development.

The 4th Lunar Month: They are very talented and ambitious in their ideals, but extremely conceited and arrogant. Consequently, they will go through lots of ups and downs, making it difficult to accomplish much in their career.

The 5th Lunar Month: Living a comfortable life, they will be blessed with a successful career in the first half of their life, but suffer from failure not long after that. In the second half of their life, they are helped by friends and others, hence enjoying quite a stable career development but without great progress.

The 6th Lunar Month: Working hard all the time, they find it difficult to live a peaceful, stable, and wealthy life. They may encounter many difficulties in their career, however, they can have a successful career if they have the will power to never concede to failure.

The 7th Lunar Month: With a smooth path throughout life, they will live comfortably, happily, peacefully, and joyfully.

The 8th Lunar Month: Bright, smart, and ambitious, they are not afraid of hardship. Therefore, they will enjoy prosperity, wealth, and respect from others throughout life.

The 9th Lunar Month: With a comfortable life that will be without serious troubles, they will be lucky and become rich.

The 10th Lunar Month: Without ideals and ambitions, they don't like to acquire knowledge, so they will leave themselves in the hands of destiny, hence living an average life.

The 11th Lunar Month: Bright, acute, and overwhelmingly talented, they have ambitions and aspirations. However, they often fall into depression since they will be on their own when it comes to achieving career development.

The 12th Lunar Month: Bright, intelligent, righteous, and honest, they tend to take action on behalf of others against injustice. They work hard all the time. Despite a comfortable life, they don't know how to enjoy it.

Overall Fortunes of the Rooster Born on Different Days by the Lunar Calendar

The 1st Day: The family will suffer from disharmony with frequent troubles. It is advisable for them to render kind deeds and accumulate virtue, which can bring about good luck.

The 2nd Day: Success can surely be made as long as they

More than Enough (Fish) Auspiciousness (Rooster)

This is one of the auspicious patterns in Chinese tradition. Auspiciousness (*ji*) sounds like Rooster while fish (*yu*) sounds like more than enough, hence denoting prosperous life in Spring Festival. It expresses the good wish of ancient people in pursuing happy and prosperous life every year.

have firm ambitions. It is not advisable to change their mind once a goal is set. Unreasonable change will lead to failure of development throughout life.

The 3rd Day: They will not be able to rely on help from relatives and parents. Despite being kind-hearted, they are not lucky people. Therefore, it is advisable for them to render good deeds and accumulate virtue.

The 4th Day: Faithful and honest, they will enjoy great fame even in their young age, in addition to a fairly good luck of wealth and a smooth road to everything.

The 5th Day: Bright and independent, they will enjoy success in doing everything, getting wealth automatically and having a pleasant marriage.

The 6th Day: With superb intelligence and thoughtfulness, they will be good at planning with little failure throughout life.

The 7th Day: Without concentrated will and resolution, they are too careful in handling things. It is advisable for them to be bold.

The 8th Day: With an unpredictable personality, they will always be of two minds, hence falling into the situation of adversity. If they have a strong will and handle things with resolution, they will enjoy great development.

The 9th Day: Suffering from poverty, hardship, and illness, they will not be able to accomplish much in their life.

The 10th Day: Talented and lucky, they are helplessly hot-tempered. They may have both success and failure in the life.

The 11th Day: Hypocritical, they cannot do things in a down-to-earth manner and lack patience, hence finding it difficult to have a successful career.

The 12th Day: They are fond of wine, women, and gambling. They can be freed from poverty and trouble if they show some restraint.

The 13th Day: With innate opportunities and great ambitions, they are loyal and honest. They will surely have success if they go for it energetically.

The 14th Day: Innately quick-tempered, they are not good at consideration and planning, hence always inviting failure.

The 15th Day: With innate wealth, they will not only enjoy fame, but also receive care from their children in their old age.

The 16th Day: They will often retreat halfway since they are not firm in handling things. They will surely have success if they have strong will-power and cultivate the spirit of enduring hardship.

The 17th Day: With innate luck, they will be blessed with family prosperity, good health, a virtuous wife and devoted children.

The 18th Day: They have ability to hold official positions and make their family proud. However, they must never be conceited and arrogant.

The 19th Day: Energetic and bright, they do things firmly and resolutely. They can have success on their own.

The 20th Day: Despite hardship in early years, they will gradually see the light in middle age and enjoy great prosperity in old age thanks to their innately firm will.

The 21st Day: Bright and smart, they are close to helpful people. With superb courage and insight, they will be famous far and wide.

The 22nd Day: They lack a sense of endurance and the spirit of bearing hardship. They will surely have success by starting from scratch if they don't lose heart in facing difficulties.

The 23rd Day: With acute intelligence and ingenious talent, they are trustworthy and have the ability to make great achievements.

The 24th Day: With no family to rely on, they are ambitious to start their own business. However, they cannot achieve what they wish due to the lack of competence.

The 25th Day: With a stable and composed personality, they have a hard time in their early years, and see a turn for the better in middle age with ample sources of wealth.

The 26th Day: With innate talent in doing business, they are blessed with a smooth path to wealth with sources of wealth coming from all directions, thus enjoying a comfortable life.

The 27th Day: With intelligence, they will surely have success if they work hard for progress.

The 28th Day: Bright, smart, and versatile, they will surely have success if they make unremitting efforts.

The Chicken Cup

With a slightly outspread opening and gradual contraction downward, it is marked by a flat bottom and crouching feet. The cup is marked by delicacy, soft, and pliable outline, straightness amidst curve, curve amidst straightness. It is solemn, charming and elegant. On the outer wall of the cup, there are two groups of chickens and hens, interspersed with lake-rocks, roses and orchids, presenting a scene of early spring. Since the Ming Dynasty, the Chicken Cup has been extremely valuable. In recent years, it has broken the record in the auction of Chinese porcelain time and again.

The 29th Day: With a sense of defending others against injustice, they are fond of solving problems, with a spirit of helping others at the expense of their own interest. They are marked by kindness and readiness to help others.

The 30th Day: They have both good and bad luck. Despite their versatile skills, they are not well-versed in any one of them due to the lack of concentration. They will surely have success if they focus professionally on advancement.

Overall Fortunes of the Rooster Born in Different Hours

11 PM–1 AM: They will be successful in their career and enjoy a comfortable life since they are helped by family. However, due to the lack of great ambition, they will not make great contributions to society.

1 AM–3 AM: Hot-tempered, bold, fierce, and righteous, they are not afraid of force or trouble and can rise courageously in sorry plight. Despite average fame in their career development, they are very popular among people exclusively due to their courage and a sense of justice, hence enjoying a satisfactory life.

3 AM–5 AM: Attractive, healthy, faithful, and honest, they will live a comfortable life.

5 AM–7 AM: Bright and smart, they are unpredictable, making it difficult for them to get along with others. They should learn more and change their temperament for a peaceful and serene life.

7 AM–9 AM: Mild and honest, they speak in conformity with what they do. However, they are very stubborn, making it difficult for them to listen to the advice of other people. They will be helped by others either in seeking for an official position or making money, so their career development will be a smooth one. They enjoy happiness and a comfortable life.

9 AM–11 AM: With sharp ups and downs, they will be apt to succeed and fail. Having been tempered through repeated failure, most of them will have success. They should ponder over

situations carefully. They should be adaptable to changes, being modest and calm. They should also maintain the same peaceful mentality either at the time of fame and prosperity or at the time of poverty, which ensures their steady development without miserable failure.

11 AM–1 PM: Bright and clever, they do things effectively, enjoying happiness and glory throughout life.

1 PM–3 PM: Versatile, intelligent, and ingenious, they will be helped by people in other places and develop their career and family away from home. With hardship in their early years, they experience a turn for the better in middle age and happiness in old age.

3 PM–5 PM: Kind-hearted, well-accomplished in learning, faithful, and devoted to their parents, they will either enjoy a high social position or gain wealth. They will receive admiration from people and be known across the country. They are blessed with peace, prosperity, and wealth until the old age.

5 PM–7 PM: Despite sharp ups and downs, they will be blessed with happiness and peace throughout life. They will be helped by family members and others, hence enjoying an official position and wealth to their satisfaction.

7 PM–9 PM: They will stay far away from home in their young age to develop their career, often resulting in quite remarkable achievements. However, they will go through many ups and downs in marriage. They should be faithful to love.

9 PM–11 PM: Bright and flexible, they will be good at running their own business. With an upright style, they will be devoted to their career. With their own intelligence and efforts, they will bring their career into the right track. In the end, they will have success and live comfortably throughout life.

Chapter Eleven
The Dog

The Dog, regarded as the animal that has a tacit agreement with human beings, is particularly faithful to mankind, hence standing for faithfulness. The Dog ranks eleventh in the Chinese zodiac and signifies "faithfulness."

Lunar Years of the Dog in the Solar Calendar

4 February 1922 to 4 February 1923

4 February 1934 to 4 February 1935

4 February 1946 to 3 February 1947

4 February 1958 to 3 February 1959

4 February 1970 to 3 February 1971

4 February 1982 to 3 February 1983

4 February 1994 to 3 February 1995

4 February 2006 to 3 February 2007

4 February 2018 to 3 February 2019

4 February 2030 to 3 February 2031

4 February 2042 to 3 February 2043

Life Path

Those born in the year of the Dog are bright and enthusiastic. Females are glamourous and attractive. They are featured by a sense of justice, affectionate with moral principles, full devotion to doing things, faithfulness, honesty, kindness, sympathy, frankness, acute intuition, and respect from other people. However, they should be careful not to be arbitrary. Otherwise, they will suffer from extremely serious setbacks.

Personality

The Dog is characterized by righteousness, courage, insight, and hot temper to some extent. They remain composed and calm when encountering emergencies. Despite their economic conditions, they pay no attention to material enjoyment and keep long term relationship with other people. Their shortcomings are marked by the inability to verbally express themselves and the tendency to do things half way.

Profession

The Dog is featured by faithfulness to their responsibility, a down-to-earth manner, hard work, an invariably strong will to overcome difficulties, and independence. They are cautious in doing everything while adhering to principles, focusing on disciplines, and advancing toward their set goals in an orderly way. They only do one or two jobs throughout life. They give priority to a sense of security and stable income while choosing their profession.

Love and Marriage

The Dog is very faithful to his spouse. Most of them will

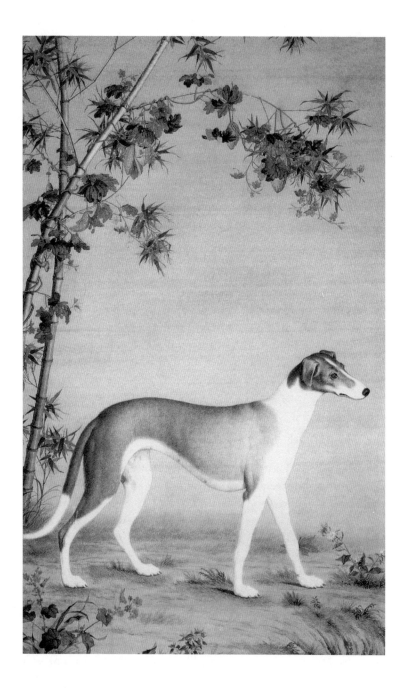

Dog Painting

This is a painting by Giuseppe Castiglione (1688—1766), an Italian painter who worked for the Qing court. He took part in the design of European-style palaces in the Old Summer Palace. Having served Emperor Kangxi, Yongzheng and Qianlong of the Qing Dynasty successively, he had been engaging in painting for over 50 years in China. Boldly blazing a new trail in exploring Western painting, he integrated Western painting with Chinese painting, having created an unprecedented painting technique and a new style.

choose people with patience as their spouse. They will spend some time getting to know the other person, taking rather long before they finally marry. Being good at knowing what other people are thinking about, they stay in harmony with others and pay attention to their family. It is suitable for them to be matched with those of the Tiger, the Rabbit, and the Horse, but they need to be careful with those of the Ox, the Dragon, the Sheep, and the Rooster.

Marriage Compatibility with Women Born in Other Animal Years

The Dog Man with the Rat Woman: This is quite an ideal match. Since the wife is mild, she can make her husband feel warm and tender in their marriage.

The Dog Man with the Ox Woman: This will not be a very harmonious marriage. Both sides need to exert tolerance and understanding for a lasting marriage.

The Dog Man with the Tiger Woman: This will be an average marriage, but life is likely to be quite plain. However, their children will be devoted to them.

The Dog Man with the Rabbit Woman: This will be a harmonious marriage. They respect each other like guests while creating a comfortable life.

The Dog Man with the Dragon Woman: They will not be able

to live together comfortably. The wife will not follow her husband blindly, hence often leading to contradictions.

The Dog Man with the Snake Woman: They will live together happily and enjoy a serene and harmonious family.

The Dog Man with the Horse Woman: This will be quite a happy marriage, with love between them and devotion from their children.

The Dog Man with the Sheep Woman: This will be quite a happy marriage, but both sides need to exert tolerance for a lasting relationship.

The Dog Man with the Monkey Woman: They will live together quite harmoniously. Both are quite realistic with mutual consent.

The Dog Man with the Rooster Woman: This will not be an ideal match, because there is a great difference between them in personality. Their relationship will take a turn for the better if one of them can exert tolerance.

The Dog Man with the Dog Woman: They will live together harmoniously, despite some small troubles between them.

The Dog Man with the Pig Woman: With a harmonious relationship, they will live together easily. Generosity is the merit that they will have in common.

Marriage Compatibility with Men Born in Other Animal Years

The Dog Woman with the Rat Man: They will live together quite happily, because both of them are ready to contribute to the marriage.

The Dog Woman with the Ox Man: There will be some difficulties since there are differences between them in views, hence understanding and tolerance is required.

The Dog Woman with the Tiger Man: They will live together harmoniously, because they share the same ideals and can strive forward together.

The Dog Woman with the Rabbit Man: This will be a happy marriage.

The Tibetan Dog

The Tibetan dog is featured by a dark yellow color on its front chest and claws which extend like big palms. Besides, its drooping upper lip covers the lower lip and that there are two nice looking big teeth upward and downward. The Tibetan dog, one of the oldest rare dogs in the world, is very adaptable to the harsh living conditions on high mountains. In Tibetan China, Nepal, and other Himalayan mountains nowadays, most of them serve as guards of temples, residences and domestic animals. Some of them travel with Tibetan traders, protecting their sheep and tents. According to the folk legend in China, Tibetan dogs are deified as the incarnation of heroically protecting the master. With protecting the master as its instinct, it is the best protector for nomads.

The Dog Woman with the Dragon Man: Their family life will not be harmonious since the wife will irritate the conceitedness of her husband.

The Dog Woman with the Snake Man: The wife feels safe with her husband since the latter is blessed with independence.

The Dog Woman with the Horse Man: Both are outgoing and

energetic, enjoying a joyful family.

The Dog Woman with the Sheep Man: Understanding and efforts are required if they want to have happiness.

The Dog Woman with the Monkey Man: This is quite a nice marriage.

The Dog Woman with the Rooster Man: This will not be an ideal marriage, hence mutual forbearance and tolerance is required.

The Dog Woman with the Dog Man: They can live together harmoniously, despite some small troubles.

The Dog Woman with the Pig Man: This will be a perfect marriage, because they are supplementary either in personality or in the trends of luck.

The Luck of Wealth

The Dog is marked by average luck of wealth, but they never waste money. They adhere to practicing economy and saving money, a spirit that they give full play to.

Overall Fortunes of the Dog in Different Animal Years

The Year of the Rat: It happens to be the year of the luck of wealth, but they have both good and bad luck in other aspects, hence more caution of unpredictable events is required.

The Year of the Ox: It is an undesirable year regarding the luck of wealth, hence more caution in verbal expression is required. They will be helped by others at the end of the year.

The Year of the Tiger: It is an undesirable year regarding the luck of wealth, hence faithfulness to their jobs is required.

The Year of the Rabbit: Blessed with great opportunities, they should render more kind deeds.

The Year of the Dragon: With obvious ups and downs in their

career, they should be careful in keeping what they have and seize the opportunity to make greater investments in start-up businesses.

The Year of the Snake: Peace will be ensured if they act in a composed manner and do not go too far in doing things.

The Year of the Horse: It is a year with great opportunities for wealth. They need to mind their health and prevent from being over exhausted.

The Year of the Sheep: Despite busy work, they gain little. Their career will be stable at the end of the year.

The Year of the Monkey: It is a year of small gains. They will encounter obstacles whenever they seek for great accomplishments.

The Year of the Rooster: They have nothing in terms of luck of wealth. They should follow the tide and render more kind deeds.

The Year of Dog: Taking defense as offense, they will have good opportunities automatically. It is advisable for them to make more good friends.

The Year of the Pig: It is advisable for them to go all out, seeking opportunities for investment and starting their own business.

Overall Fortunes of the Dog Born in Different Months by the Lunar Calendar

The 1st Lunar Month: Without obvious ups and downs, they will live a plain but comfortable life.

The 2nd Lunar Month: Life is with both joy and worry. They are often self-centered, hence inviting disgust from many people and lots of troubles. However, they will be helped by others after middle age. There won't be serious disasters.

The 3rd Lunar Month: Being versatile, they enjoy quite a happy life. They need to make more friends so as to accumulate more wealth.

The 4th Lunar Month: Without great ambitions, they are content with life. They are friendly and kind with many friends.

They live comfortably and enjoy peace throughout life.

The 5th Lunar Month: In their young age, they have a well-off family. In middle age, they gradually experience a turn for the better and some accomplishments in their career. The older they are, the richer they will be.

The 6th Lunar Month: With acute thinking, an outgoing personality, and good health, they have great ambitions, but they are quite difficult to be realized since they do not have good luck .

The 7th Lunar Month: They are marked by firmness, tenderness, and righteousness. Things will start going smooth around forty years old and they will live a stable life.

The 8th Lunar Month: With overwhelming talents, they enjoy rapid career development, desirable luck of wealth, as well as a comfortable and prosperous life.

The 9th Lunar Month: Living a comfortable and prosperous life, they are independent, resolute, resourceful, and ambitious. They need to safeguard the self-respect of other people.

The 10th Lunar Month: Righteous and talented, they encounter quite a lot of setbacks in their young age, but see a turn for the better around thirty years old with a stable family and career.

The 11th Lunar Month: They will see a turn for the better after twenty-five years old and a big turn for the better after seventy years old. However, their luck is just average in middle age.

The 12th Lunar Month: They will enjoy the happiness of a family bond and live happily throughout their life. They will have great achievements in their career.

Overall Fortunes of the Dog Born on Different Days by the Lunar Calendar

The 1st Day: Marked by honesty, a sense of justice, and sympathy, they enjoy wealth of all kinds.

The 2nd Day: Mild and honest, they are fond of accumulating virtue and rendering kind deeds.

Dog-Shaped Jade Pendant

Length: 5.7 cm. Width: 3.5 cm. Thickness: 0.5 cm. Color: dark green.
Ornamental jade in the Late Shang Dynasty
Tomb of Fuhao, Anyang, Henan Province
Archeological Research Institute under Chinese Academy of Social Science

Just like a dog or a wolf, it crouches down while looking back. This jade pendant is marked by round eyes, ears leaning back, protruding buttocks, short front and rear legs, front legs under the neck, bent rear legs and a drooping long tail. Its neck is decorated with overlapped patterns while its body is featured by deformed cloud patterns, with the same patterns on both sides. Its front and rear hoofs are brightly polished, with the tail protruding a slant blade. There is a small hole respectively on its upper lip and its front hoof. The hole on the lip is seen in the middle of the body for balancing the object strung through. It can serve both as a pendant and a carving knife.

The 3rd Day: Despite being bright and open-minded, they are weak in forbearance. They pay attention to brotherhood and belittle other women. They have quite a desirable luck of wealth.

The 4th Day: With undesirable luck of wealth and less gains in their early years, they are helped by others with their career accomplishments. They will enjoy both fame and gain.

The 5th Day: Hot-tempered, they suffer from more illness due to their hard work. Their good luck will appear if they can stay calm and composed.

The 6th Day: Bright and virtuous, they can become famous. The male is helped by his wife, while the female benefits from a nice husband.

The 7th Day: In good health, they have access to wealth and prosperity.

The 8th Day: Bright, energetic, resourceful, firm, resolute, and independent, they will surely enjoy success.

The 9th Day: Working hard in their early years, they have no access to wealth. They will see a turn for the better in middle age with great career development.

The 10th Day: Smart, flexible, energetic, and adaptable to changes, they can have success independently.

The 11th Day: Outspoken and good at verbal expression, they have a sense of vanity. They will surely have success in establishing a family and career if they can form will power.

The 12th Day: They find it difficult to develop their career in the early years, but enjoy stability and prosperity in middle age. They will be helped by children and live happily in old age.

The 13th Day: They will not have access to good luck or help in their early years despite their outstanding talents, hence independence and hard work is required.

The 14th Day: They will not have access to good luck in their early years and see a turn for the better in middle age. They will have to start from the ground up.

The 15th Day: Bright, eager to learn, and versatile, they make their own way and start from the ground up.

The 16th Day: With innate talents and accomplishments in academic study, they can have success if they strive forward gradually.

The 17th Day: Bright and smart, they can have success. They will enjoy power, influence, and wealth.

The 18th Day: Outspoken and impatient, they have fewer successes and more failures despite their hard work.

The 19th Day: Kind, faithful, honest, and generous, they will often be helped by others with good luck of success.

The 20th Day: With a sharp tongue, a soft heart, and righteousness, they are fond of making friends and live a considerably happy life after middle age.

The 21st Day: Flexible, resourceful, and well-versed in verbal expression, they are marked by leadership and the momentum of a general, with the prospect of making great accomplishments.

The 22nd Day: With a strong personality and hot-temper, they refuse to listen to the opinions of other people, hence finding it difficult to make great accomplishments.

The 23rd Day: Their intelligence is beneficial to their development in business but not in politics. With good luck of wealth, they will enjoy prosperity.

The 24th Day: With innate intelligence, they can have success in their career with great fame, bringing honor to their families.

The 25th Day: With lots of difficulties as well as ups and downs happening sometimes in their early years, they will enjoy sweetness after bitterness.

The 26th Day: With innate good luck, they are agreeable and respectable.

The 27th Day: With sweetness coming after bitterness, they see a turn for the better in middle age with great career development. They will have success, fame, and wealth as well as harmonious marriage.

The 28th Day: Blessed with talents, they will surely enjoy power and respect and have a prosperous family and career.

The 29th Day: Well-educated, talented, and enterprising, they are marked by an excessively strong personality and distrust in others, which unavoidably leads to conflicts with people.

The 30th Day: With more joy and less worry, they will enjoy

a nice marriage and career along with wealth. They will have prosperous family and career.

Overall Fortunes of the Dog Born in Different Hours

11 PM–1 AM: Nothing is advantageous in their pursuit. They will drift along in a very awkward situation.

1 AM–3 AM: There will be many troubles and unexpected things. As luck would have it, they will be helped by others, hence enjoying some peace.

3 AM–5 AM: They will often encounter setbacks, hence requiring caution at all times.

5 AM–7 AM: They will suffer from minor illnesses and the loss of small amounts of wealth, but without serious troubles.

7 AM–9 AM: As their attitude with money is marked by "easy come and easy go," they will fail to keep their wealth.

9 AM–11 AM: Because of the help from others, they will be free from serious troubles.

11 AM–1 PM: With power in hand, they will be famous. However, greediness and people with ulterior motives will lead to failure.

1 PM–3 PM: Despite having to do everything themselves, they will enjoy a smooth road without any difficulties.

3 PM–5 PM: It will be suitable for them to develop their career away from home to realize their objectives and aspirations.

5 PM–7 PM: They will be much troubled by illnesses because of not being in good health.

7 PM–9 PM: Despite being intelligent and versatile, they will encounter setbacks in the year of the Dog.

9 PM–11 PM: In spite of drifting away from home, they will enjoy a bright future.

Chapter Twelve
The Pig

The Pig is honest, mild, and peaceful. It never hurts others, but instead, brings economic benefit to people, becoming the piggy bank of farmers. Therefore, the Pig ranks twelfth in the Chinese zodiac and represents "popularity among people."

Lunar Years of the Pig in the Solar Calendar

5 February 1923 to 4 February 1924

5 February 1935 to 4 February 1936

4 February 1947 to 4 February 1948

4 February 1959 to 4 February 1960

4 February 1971 to 4 February 1972

4 February 1983 to 3 February 1984

4 February 1995 to 3 February 1996

4 February 2007 to 3 February 2008

4 February 2019 to 3 February 2020

4 February 2031 to 3 February 2032

4 February 2043 to 3 February 2044

Life Path

The Pig is sincere and righteous with a strong sense of justice, straightforwardness, earnestness in doing things, kindness, generosity, and greatly popular among people. They treat people with consistent loyalty and thoughtfulness throughout life. People feel all the more attached to them since they put a lot of value in friendship. The Pig is very particular about decency. They look imposing, like a knight while possessing the fine quality of being ready to help others as knights do. They will never stand by if they can help others. This characteristic brings deep respect to them and makes them self-confident to continuously create one wonder after another. Meanwhile, the frankness and sincerity of the Pig can win help from all people who will do so automatically without their request for it.

Personality

The Pig is composed and strong-willed while also naive, romantic, outgoing, and mild. Marked by great concentration, once the objective is set, they will go all out to reach it, but they should overcome the defect of getting angry easily.

Profession

The Pig is hardworking throughout life. They work strenuously in all kinds of activities. They will try all they can to make a success of any job assigned to them with an indomitable spirit and great courage. The result is always perfect. Therefore, full confidence should be rendered to those born in the year of the Pig to let them strive for accomplishment.

Paper Cutting Pasting on Window: *A Fat Pig Trying to Push the Door Open*

As a Chinese folk saying goes, "The advent of a Dog signifies poverty while the advent of a Pig denotes wealth." On every first day of the first lunar month, most families are fond of pasting paper-cuts with Pig as the motif respectively on the left and right glass-windows of their house, wishing to have the advent of wealth. *A Fat Pig Trying to Push the Door Open* is the most typical. The Pig is valued by farmers as it is always associated with harvest and prosperity. It can give birth to lots of children, hence constituting the auspiciousness of prosperous wealth and endless propagation. This paper cutting pattern also foretells a bumper harvest next year.

Love and Marriage

They are blessed with a very smooth love life and a peaceful family life. Those who are married enjoy harmony and happiness while the unmarried will meet good marriage prospects at any time. It is suitable for those of the Pig to be matched with those of the Tiger, the Sheep and the Rabbit, but they should be careful in their match with those of the Snake, the Monkey, and the Pig.

Marriage Compatibility with Women Born in Other Animal Years

The Pig Man with the Rat Woman: This will be a perfect marriage, as long as the wife is not too unrestrained.

The Pig Man with the Ox Woman: It will be very difficult for them to get the warmth, affection and love since both sides will seek for relationships outside the marriage.

The Pig Man with the Tiger Woman: They will live together harmoniously, but the wife should be careful not to be too fascinated with her husband.

The Pig Man with the Rabbit Woman: This will be a perfect marriage. They respect each other like guests and do things in concert. Their children are devoted to them.

The Pig Man with the Dragon Woman: They can live together, but the wife is too extroverted. So, her husband should be tolerant.

The Pig Man with the Snake Woman: This will not be a suitable marriage. The husband needs to adapt himself to his wife, but he will complain in days to come.

The Pig Man with the Horse Woman: Due to the differences in personalities, they will not live together happily, hence requiring mutual tolerance and support.

The Pig Man with the Sheep Woman: The personality and talents of the husband will make his wife feel happy and satisfied.

The Pig Man with the Monkey Woman: Their marriage will be average, since the husband has a sense of crisis marked by perplexity about how to establish the authorities as a husband.

The Pig Man with the Rooster Woman: The tolerance and thoughtfulness of the husband makes his wife feel joyful.

The Pig Man with the Dog Woman: This will naturally be a perfect marriage, because both understand and trust each other.

The Pig Man with the Pig Woman: With both good and bad luck, this will either be a desirable marriage or a miserable one, hence concerted effort is required.

Marriage Compatibility with Men Born in Other Animal Years

The Pig Woman with the Rat Man: They will live together harmoniously and happily, sharing prosperity and glory.

The Pig Woman with the Ox Man: The husband is very attracted to his wife.

The Pig Woman with the Tiger Man: They understand and admire each other, and have enough energy to take care of each other.

The Pig Woman with the Rabbit Man: This will be a happy marriage with devoted children.

The Pig Woman with the Dragon Man: This will be quite a harmonious marriage. The wife knows how to take care of her husband.

The Pig Woman with the Snake Man: This will not be a suitable marriage, since the husband will not be accustomed to the personality of his wife.

The Pig Woman with the Horse Man: They can live together, but there will be small frictions which require adjustment in order to achieve harmony.

The Pig Woman with the Sheep Man: They can live together. Both sides are thoughtful, hence enjoying a lasting relationship.

The Pig Woman with the Monkey Man: The wife will be tolerant if her husband does not go too far.

The Pig Woman with the Rooster Man: This will not be an ideal marriage, since the over-fastidiousness of the wife will annoy her husband.

The Pig Woman with the Dog Man: This will be a harmonious marriage. They live happily with many children.

The Pig Woman with the Pig Man: It is difficult for them to understand each other throughout life and they won't interfere with each other. There will be a lasting relationship if they try to avoid quarrels.

The Luck of Wealth

They have quite an ideal life with steady economic growth and comfortable living conditions. However, while making investments in their career, they should also make investments in financial management, enhance the level of management, and make progress steadily.

Overall Fortunes of the Pig in Different Animal Years

The Year of the Rat: They will encounter difficulties while seeking for wealth through business. However, they will be helped by others in the face of difficulties.

The Year of the Ox: They will enjoy a prosperous business and ample sources of wealth. Though there will be small obstacles and small loss of wealth in the middle of the year, it will not matter much. They should render more good deeds.

The Year of the Tiger: Encountering many unexpected things, they will always find themselves in adverse situations. If living at a place in the southeast, they will experience more luck and get help from others.

The Year of the Rabbit: They will gain wealth through the right channels. However, they will be apt to come across troubles after the summer, hence requiring caution to avoid adversities and seek for benefit.

The Year of the Dragon: With quite desirable luck in getting an official position and developing their career, they will also seek for employment away from home along with many happy tidings. However, they will not be in good health, hence leading to insubstantial fame easily and the loss of wealth which frees them from troubles.

The Year of the Snake: Seeking for employment away from home, they will be apt to change professions. Speculation will surely bring them some gains. They should be careful about their health and the health of their family members. The loss of wealth can free them from troubles.

The Year of the Horse: They will enjoy ample wealth and profits. Despite troubles, they will be helped by others, hence turning bad luck into opportunities. They will stay safe and sound with the advent of glad tidings if they can nip problems in the bud.

The Year of the Sheep: They will enjoy quite desirable trends of luck and get twice the results with half of their efforts. They will have many good luck, fame, and success. However, they should be careful not to stay away from home too often and not to change professions. Otherwise, there will be more bad luck and less opportunities.

The Year of the Monkey: They should be cautious. Health and peace are the most important things.

The Year of the Rooster: With undesirable luck of wealth and loss of wealth, they will work hard to little avail. They should only seek for fame instead of wealth this year.

The Year of the Dog: The luck is just average at the beginning of the year, but they see a turn for the better in the middle of the year. As they are helped by others, they will avoid adversities and get benefit as well as turn chaos into peace with quite a lot of gains.

The Year of the Pig: It will be disadvantageous when mixing with wrong friends and there will be ups and downs in their career development. The luck of wealth is average. Therefore, they should be cautious in making investments to avoid complete loss. Stability comes first.

Jade Pig of the Han Dynasty

This is a quite commonly seen funeral jade ware to be grasped by the hand or worn. In ancient times, the Pig stood for wealth. The number of pigs served to demonstrate the extent of wealth of a family at that time. Pottery pigs and pig-shaped pots were unearthed from the tombs of the New Stone Age. Jade carved into pigs as funeral objects signified the ample wealth brought by the deceased into another world. This is a jade pig from the Han Dynasty. Jade pigs of this kind were seen mostly in the tombs from the Han Dynasty, generally in the hand of the deceased as a funeral object.

Overall Fortunes of the Pig Born in Different Months by the Lunar Calendar

The 1st Lunar Month: They are composed with a strong will. They are upright and fond of criticizing others and lack forbearance. Also, they are very dependent and unsociable.

The 2nd Lunar Month: Innately bright, virtuous, and energetic, they are able to make great accomplishments with opportunities throughout life.

The 3rd Lunar Month: They will be in good health. However, they will not be on good terms with others due to their stubborn personality. They are respected thanks to their noble ambition.

The 4th Lunar Month: Innately bright, they possess the talent of leadership. They have many benefactors. They will not make great accomplishments unless they act in a down-to-earth manner.

The 5th Lunar Month: They are mild with some minor talents, enabling them to have success in art and literature. However, they will not make great accomplishments due to the lack of courage and resourcefulness. Being conservative throughout life, they will gradually enjoy happiness in old age.

The 6th Lunar Month: Despite great talents and immense knowledge, they can accomplish nothing due to their instinctive laziness.

The 7th Lunar Month: Living a comfortable life, they are arbitrary people. They will surely have success since they enjoy a smooth road everywhere they go.

The 8th Lunar Month: As authorities, they will become leaders with fame, success, and respect from other people. However, they should make gradual progress through hardship.

The 9th Lunar Month: Enjoying a comfortable life, prosperity, and glory without any worries, they will be popular among people and receive praise from the public.

The 10th Lunar Month: Righteous and respectful, they will enjoy prosperity and success in their thriving old age.

The 11th Lunar Month: They are apt to get angry and stubborn. However, they respect themselves and make themselves happy. They have both fame and gain, free from worries throughout life.

The 12th Lunar Month: Despite living a comfortable life free from worries, they will not be lucky in getting official positions. There will be more bad luck and less opportunities. Though they are talented, it will not be of any use.

Money Box (*Pu Man*)

This was a container for saving money in ancient China, similar to the piggybank used by people in modern times. The round coins with a square in the center were popular for over 2,000 years in ancient China. For the convenience of saving money, our ancestors made pot-shaped or box-shaped pottery containers with a narrow opening on the top for copper coins to be put in. There was only an opening without exit. Such pots would be broken when they were full of coins. *Pu man* means that they would be broken when they were full. In modern times, *pu man* often takes the form of the Pig, denoting expectation of wealth.

Overall Fortunes of the Pig Born on Different Days by the Lunar Calendar

The 1st Day: With quite a desirable career and luck of wealth, they will enjoy prosperity and glory despite the lack of family help.

The 2nd Day: The man indulges in wine and women, finding it difficult to make great accomplishments. The woman's fate is quite auspicious with many good luck.

The 3rd Day: With both auspiciousness and bad luck throughout life, they will enjoy quite good luck in career and wealth, but they need to mind lawsuits.

The 4th Day: Innately bright, they will be helped by others with good luck in official positions, career, and wealth, hence living a comfortable life free from worries.

The 5th Day: Despite working hard, they will not have many achievements. It is just like walking in the rain at night with a bleak future.

The 6th Day: Innately smart and honest, they will be on good terms with other people in addition to accomplishments in their career.

The 7th Day: With innate leadership, they will be admired by people with the prospect of making great accomplishments.

The 8th Day: They enjoy luck when it comes to getting official positions. However, they fail to treat others mildly, hence having many opponents and inviting jealousy.

The 9th Day: Despite hardship for a time, they can enjoy a smooth path thanks to their intelligence and wisdom.

The 10th Day: Flexible and talented, they will have great accomplishments. However, they should pay attention to cultivating cultural accomplishment and overcome conceitedness.

The 11th Day: Despite a bright future, they will need to work hard for gains and accomplishment after overcoming difficulties.

The 12th Day: Suffering from adversities in the first half of their life, they will see a turn for the better in the second half, with opportunities and satisfaction.

The 13th Day: They should pay attention to getting along with other people, never acting at will. They should wait for the opportunity to demonstrate amazing achievements.

The 14th Day: They will be apt to be arrogant in their young age, with undesirable luck. There will be a turn for the better after middle age.

The 15th Day: They will be in a sorry plight and will surely have success if they possess superb will-power and a fighting spirit.

The 16th Day: They will enjoy success and fame throughout life. However, it is not proper for them to get married early and that their children will be apt to stay far away from home.

The 17th Day: Blessed with intelligence, courage, talent, virtue, and prestige, they will surely enjoy great fame and gains in their life.

The 18th Day: With innate talents in art, they will surely have accomplishments if they work hard.

The 19th Day: With sweetness coming after bitterness, they work hard at a young age and begin to see a turn for the better in their middle age, enjoying prosperity and glory throughout life.

The 20th Day: The woman's fate will be brighter. Pig women are talented in art, well-read, and outstanding in academics. They will surely enjoy fame and success if they know how to make progress.

The 21st Day: Particularly bright and outstandingly talented, they possess the ability of judgment and leadership. They will be popular among people and surely experience great accomplishments if they are modest.

The 22nd Day: Despite being versatile, they fail almost every time in their efforts due to the lack of concentration. They may have success if they concentrate on making progress.

The 23rd Day: With help from older relatives and others, they will be likely to have a successful career. They will surely have success if they double their efforts and lay a solid foundation.

The 24th Day: With innate talents, they are willing to help others, hence deserving respect as well as gaining reputation and wealth.

The 25th Day: With both auspiciousness and bad luck throughout life, they will be apt to gain fame and experience success in the first half of their life, but lose it all in the second half. Also, they should be on the alert against people with ulterior motives.

The 26th Day: Weak-willed and without self-confidence, they will find it hopeless to accomplish anything. They should make more efforts in cultivating their will-power to experience a turn for the better.

The 27th Day: They will be apt to indulge in wine and women as well as quarrel with others. They will not be able to extricate themselves from plight unless they are helped by others.

The 28th Day: Marked by an unpredictable personality and unsettled ambition, they tend to change their minds for objectives beyond their reach. They will surely have success if they concentrate on specific career developments.

The 29th Day: Innately lucky, they won't have to worry about their future. They enjoy a smooth career, prosperity, and ample wealth.

The 30th Day: With superb intelligence, thoughtful ideas, and expertise in planning, they will enjoy a successful career. They will have fame and power throughout life.

Overall Fortunes of the Pig Born in Different Hours

11 PM–1 AM: With a handsome and attractive appearance, they are romantic, bright, spruce, mild, sentimental, and loose in contacting people of the opposite sex. They will get into unnecessary trouble if they don't exert restraint over themselves.

1 AM–3 AM: As they are born in an era that is disadvantageous to them, they will have to work hard to start their career and work strenuously throughout life.

3 AM–5 AM: Hot-tempered, bold, courageous, and conceited,

they are fond of being self-centered. They must cultivate accomplishments if they want to succeed.

5 AM–7 AM: With family help and assistance from others, they will experience rapid development in their career, either becoming wealthy men quickly or becoming outstanding in an official position. They will have prosperity and glory throughout life.

7 AM–9 AM: Kind-hearted, they are fond of rendering good deeds. They will live happily throughout life.

9 AM–11 AM: Hot-tempered, strong-willed, and resolute in doing things, they are quite arbitrary. Developing their career away from home, they will be helped by others, hence being able to experience success. However, they should be mindful of big ups and downs.

11 AM–1 PM: They are fond of study, making it suitable for them to become officials. However, it is not suitable for them to do business or engage in enterprises due to their undesirable luck of wealth.

1 PM–3 PM: Bright, smart, and extremely flexible, they will be famous, making their family proud. However, they will be apt to arouse jealousy and hatred of people with ulterior motives.

3 PM–5 PM: Quite well-grounded in family wealth, they will also be helped by others, hence living a happy and peaceful life.

5 PM–7 PM: Without any help in their career, they will encounter many difficulties. However, they will surely have great accomplishments in their career if they rely on their endurance and carry on with it to the end.

7 PM–9 PM: They enjoy many glad tidings, satisfactory love, and success in their career. They will have many children and lots of good luck. They should pay attention to their physical health and exercise regularly.

9 PM–11 PM: They will start a business by completely relying on their intelligence, wisdom, and the spirit of endurance. They will enjoy a comfortable life free from worries despite only a few sources of wealth.

Appendix

Dates of the Chinese Dynasties

Xia Dynasty (夏)···2070–1600 BC
Shang Dynasty (商)···1600–1046 BC
Zhou Dynasty (周)···1046–256 BC
    Western Zhou Dynasty (西周)··1046–771 BC
    Eastern Zhou Dynasty (东周)··770–256 BC
       Spring and Autumn Period (春秋)·····························770–476 BC
       Warring States Period (战国)···································475–221 BC
Qin Dynasty (秦)··221–206 BC
Han Dynasty (汉)···206 BC–220 AD
    Western Han Dynasty (西汉)···206 BC–25 AD
    Eastern Han Dynasty (东汉)···25–220
Three Kingdoms (三国)···220–280
    Wei (魏)··220–265
    Shu Han (蜀)··221–263
    Wu (吴)··222–280
Jin Dynasty (晋)···265–420
    Western Jin Dynasty (西晋)··265–316
    Eastern Jin Dynasty (东晋)···317–420
Northern and Southern Dynasties (南北朝)·································420–589
    Southern Dynasties (南朝)···420–589
    Liang Dynasty (梁)··502–557
    Northern Dynasties (北朝)···439–581
Sui Dynasty (隋)···581–618
Tang Dynasty (唐)··618–907
Five Dynasties and Ten Kingdoms (五代十国)··························907–960
    Five Dynasties (五代)···907–960
    Ten Kingdoms (十国)···902–979
Song Dynasty (宋)··960–1279
    Northern Song Dynasty (北宋)···960–1127
    Southern Song Dynasty (南宋)·······································1127–1279
Liao Dynasty (辽)···916–1125
Jin Dynasty (金)···1115–1234
Xixia Dynasty (or Tangut) (西夏)··1038–1227
Yuan Dynasty (元)···1279–1368
Ming Dynasty (明)···1368–1644
Qing Dynasty (清)··1644–1911